GW00482175

Words The Vikings Gave Us

Muriel

Grace Tierney

Also by Grace Tierney

Nonfiction

"How To Get Your Name In The Dictionary"
"Words The Sea Gave Us"

Fiction

"Hamster Stew & Other Stories"
"Nit Roast & Other Stories"
"The Librarian's Secret Diary"

First published by Wordfoolery Press, 2021

Cover Design by Peter Sheehan Studio

ISBN-13: 978-1999977641

Contents

Introduction

Tall, blonde, and adventurous, the Vikings came from Norway, Denmark, and Sweden and from 750-1066 A.D. they changed everywhere they landed in their longships.

I've been exploring the origins of English words and phrases in my weekly Wordfoolery blog for more than 12 years now but it wasn't until I wrote my book "Words The Sea Gave Us" and researched the ship-building and navigation innovations of the Vikings that I realised the sheer range of words the English dictionary has inherited from them.

Without Vikings we wouldn't have simple everyday words like *they, big, take,* and *get.* Our romantic lives would be poorer without *honeymoon, hug, kiss, husband,* and *happy.* Yes, Vikings did a certain amount of raiding and you'll find *bash, shield maiden, anger, gun, berserk,* and *ransack* in the Fight like a Viking chapter, but Vikings were settlers and farmers too, as reflected in *cart, flock, muck,* and *smithy.*

It's often assumed that Vikings came, raided, and left but their history was written by the very monks whose monasteries they destroyed. Understandably that led to a certain amount of bias and confusion, although the "Vikings" and "Lost Kingdom" TV series have tried to balance the scales.

The Vikings were part of a complex hierarchical society. They travelled from America to Russia and the Arctic to Africa. The Byzantine Emperor had Viking bodyguards. The Vikings had surprisingly modern attitudes to women's rights (see the Norse Romance and Fight Like a

Viking chapters) and they influenced the power structures and royal dynasties of Europe (see the Power & Politics chapter).

Did you know Vikings ruled over *Orkney* and *Shetland* (islands now part of the United Kingdom) for nearly 700 years? That's three centuries longer than the Romans ruled Britain. Even now 60% of *Orkney* islanders are genetically linked to Norway. I explore that and other geographical stories in the Viking Place Names chapter.

The Vikings changed the face of Europe, especially northern Europe, as much as the Romans did. As well as giving us *Thor* in the Marvel universe, Abba and *IKEA*, and inspiring Tolkien's "Lord of the Rings" (arguably inspiring the entire genre of epic fantasy in the process), they've bequeathed more words to the English language than you might expect. Modern sounding words such as *bug, thing,* and *bash* all came from the Vikings.

In England for 160 years (880-1042 A.D.), the Danelaw treaties permitted Viking settlement and government of land from York to London including the East Midlands, Suffolk, Norfolk, Cambridge, Essex, and more. 35,000 Danish Vikings moved to England, equalling the population of London at that time. From 1016-1042 England was ruled entirely by a Viking king, Cnut the Great, and his descendants, in a realm which united Denmark, England, and Norway in the North Sea Empire. Not an empire I found mentioned in any of my old schoolbooks.

During the Danelaw years Old Norse mingled with Anglo Saxon easily as they are both from the same linguistic family (Proto-Germanic). In many cases the Anglo Saxons had a word for an object or action yet within a century or two that term died away and the Old Norse word, perhaps with a spelling change, had completely replaced the original.

By 1000 A.D. Old Norse (or the Danish tongue as it was called) was the most widely spoken language in Europe thanks to the Swedes, Norwegians, Icelanders, and Danes who had spread it west to Leif Erickson's Vinland colony (in modern-day Canada), east to the Volga River (in modern-day Russia), and as far south as Spain, Italy, and northern Africa.

Roughly 600 Viking words are in common use in English today and thousands more persist in dialect words, such as *kirk* in Scotland.

This Viking word journey will take us from Invading the Menu to Farming, Fighting, Zoology, and Myths. Surprising stops on the route include Norse Romance (*hugs* and *kisses*, anybody?), Power & Politics (*laws, ombudsman,* and the oldest parliament in the world), Modern Vikings (*quisling, noble, skype,* and *bluetooth*), and finally at stop at the Salmagundi chapter for Vikings words which defy categorisation (*frisbee, litmus,* and *plogging*) but that are simply too much fun to exclude.

Don your helmet, grab your axe, and may Odin bless our voyage into the Words The Vikings Gave Us.

1. Invading the Menu

Vikings are best known for sailing off in longships to raid or settle around Europe and further afield but they were also farmers and cooks. Viking culinary history contributed several dishes and words to the English language.

Historians believe that one of the main reasons those Viking raids began was because they struggled to grow enough crops along the fjords to sustain their population during the long and harsh Scandinavian winters. Once the raiders saw the richness of the land elsewhere, especially in England, they were keen to settle. As a boat-load of farmers on their summer break they knew good land when they saw it.

Vikings typically ate twice a day – once in the morning (leftover stew plus bread and fruit) and once again in the evening (fish or meat stew served with ale or mead) after the day's work was done.

On special days those meals would be expanded to feast level, depending on the wealth of the family. They might add roasted meats and larger helpings all round. If they'd brought back any unusual foods from their trips, that is when they would be served.

Few recipes of the period exist but dishes they are believed to have eaten include rye bread and meatballs. Yes, Swedish meatballs pre-date IKEA stores.

The most obvious Norse additions to English in the kitchen are *gravalax* and the *smorgasbord* but they also gave us *keg* (handy for your ale or mead for the feast), *egg, whisk, steak*, and even *cake.*

Barmy

Barmy may not be something you can eat, but its links to the Viking menu are strong enough to land it a spot in this chapter.

To describe somebody as *barmy* in British English is to say they are foolish or crazy. *Barmy* is an adjective form of the noun *barm* – the froth on yeasty malt liquor, typically during the creation of beer or ale. The bubbly *barm* was also used to leaven bread and certain cakes. Both jobs would have been common on Viking-era farms and for many centuries thereafter, so it's no surprise that *barm* comes from an Old Norse word *barmr* (froth).

Barm entered Old English as *beorma* to mean either yeast or the head of a beer, again with that frothy meaning. It is likely the Vikings brought the word to English.

The Viking influence on English was particularly strong in northern English because it was a centre for their settlements and population. Viking footprints on *barm* are easily spotted in *barm cake*. This cake, from north-west England, leavened with *barm,* is a soft, rounded, flattish bread roll.

Another *barm*-related recipe is that for *barmbrack* (sometimes mis-named barnbrack) – the traditional Halloween cake in Ireland. The *barmbrack* (*bairín breac* in Irish which translates as speckled loaf) is a round fruit cake leavened with yeast or *barm* which is usually served sliced and buttered. Traditionally items were baked inside the dough and receiving one in your slice was deemed to be a primitive form of fortune telling. The dried pea predicted you wouldn't marry that year, the stick foretold an unhappy marriage, the rag suggested poverty, the coin claimed future wealth, and finding the ring assured you of a wedding before the next Halloween.

Wales has a similar fruit bread called *bara brith*, but without the surprise ingredients and fortune telling.

It wasn't until the 1800s that *barmy* gained the additional meaning of foolish or mad from its connection to frothy, bubbly behaviour.

Cake

It's hard to imagine fierce Vikings blowing out the candles on their birthday *cake* while their companions sing a little song, but without them the English language wouldn't have the word *cake*.

Well, they might have had *coecel* instead as that was the Old English word which was replaced by the Old Norse import, *kaka*. *Kaka* described a flat mass of baked dough. It wouldn't be until the early 1400s that *cakes* became a light mixture of flour, sugar, and butter so that Viking birthday *kaka* wasn't what we'd eat on a birthday these days.

Kaka is related to Middle Dutch (*koke*), Dutch (*koek* – cake, gingerbread, or dumpling), and German *Kuchen* (*cake* or tart).

The idea of *taking the cake* as being the best arose in the 1800s, *piece of cake* being something easy is American English from 1936 and as you probably know the idea of *letting them eat cake* wasn't from Marie Antoinette. It was used in Rousseau's "Confessions" in 1740 and had been associated with many other princesses and queens before her.

Dregs

Vikings, like other nationalities of the time, loved to brew mead so it's perhaps unsurprising that they provided the word *dregs* to the English language.

The *dregs* are the sediment and residue left at the bottom of a vessel after the fermentation process. Typically this is strained away by some physical or chemical process when brewing beer or making wine. The Vikings provided this to English brewers around 1300 from the Old Norse word *dregg* (sediment) which comes from a Germanic root word for making something muddy.

By the 1500s the *dregs* was being used to describe anything worthless or useless and this is the more common use of the word in modern English.

Egg

Egg is a surprisingly late addition to the English language considering how common it is as a foodstuff in history. Old English had the word *aeg* from a Proto-Germanic root but then it met with *egg* from Old Norse (and ultimately the same root word). *Egg* became the more popular word in northern England by the mid 1300s but it wasn't until Middle English and about 1500 that *egg* won the battle and *aeg* was lost to the English language.

The English verb to *egg*, as in to *egg on* (1500s) or incite, dates to the 1200s and is a direct borrowing from Norse (*eggja*).

Full

If you've drunk or eaten to your complete satisfaction you are *full* and you've the Old Norse word *fullr* to thank for it. *Full* is the Old English adjective spelling but *ful*, with only a single L, was the adverb form and it was widely used. It was used to describe an action as being very or complete. For example you might know *full well* that you'd eaten too much roast beef for dinner.

Full moon is related to the sense of completion, as was *full house* which was a theatrical term for having sold all the seats in the audience (1710) long before it was ever a way to describe a good hand in poker (1887).

Gravlax

Gravlax is a popular Nordic dish of raw salmon cured in salt, sugar, and dill. The salmon is thinly-sliced and usually served as an opening dish with dill and mustard sauce, either on bread or with boiled potatoes.

Gravlax is a compound Scandinavian word of *grave* (or *gräva*) and *lax* (salmon) – literally *grave fish*. *Grave* in this case relates to digging a trench in the ground and is linguistically related to *grave*. The traditional method (now not used for valid food poisoning concerns) was to wrap the fish in birch bark and bury it where the wet cold conditions combined with lack of oxygen caused it to ferment. It also used the bare minimum of salt, a valuable commodity, and preserved the fish for the long, cold winters. The burial and fermentation is not part of modern *gravlax* recipes.

Keg

Keg, as in a barrel of beer, has been an English word since the 1600s but came from an earlier addition to the language, *kag* from the mid 1400s. *Kag* came from Old Norse *kaggi* (*keg* or cask). You'll find similar words in other Scandinavian tongues such as *kagge* in Swedish and *kagg* in Norwegian.

Rotten

Food *rotted* easily in Viking times. In an era before canning and fridges they used salting, smoking, and fermentation to preserve enough food to last them through the long, dark winters. None of those methods are perfect so it is perhaps unsurprising that *rotten* entered English from a Scandinavian source around 1300. The likely root is the Old Norse word *rotinn* (decayed) from the verb *rotna* (to decay).

The concept of something *rotten* being corrupt arose in the late 1300s and by 1528 the language had the idea of a *rotten* apple corrupting those around it.

Scales

While the *scales* of a fish came to English from French and the *musical scales* came from the Romans, *weighing scales* came to English with the Vikings.

To understand the origin of the word you need to forget the digital *scales* in your kitchen and think about the old-fashioned kind, the suspended pair of bowls held aloft by statues of Justice, where the user put the item to be weighed in one bowl and added known weights to the other bowl until they balanced.

Scales entered English from Old Norse *skal* (bowl or drinking cup). The cups for drinking were similar to the cups on the balanced *scales*, presumably, and the word stuck. A similar process gave Dutch and German their words for the same things. It may even go back to the idea of shellfish shells (which are often a pair of bowl-shaped structures) perhaps because they would have been used as simple drinking vessels by coastal dwellers such as the Vikings.

By the 1400s, *scales* were more commonly used to describe the *scales*, or the pans of those *scales*, rather than drinking cups. By the 1600s, *scales* were also being used to describe the zodiac constellation, Libra, whose symbol is a set of weighing balance *scales*.

The Viking link of *scales* to drinking persists to this day in the common Scandinavian toast *Skol!* (or *skål*) which originated with the Vikings. Visitors to Scandinavia should take this toast seriously. Eye-contact with each member of the group by the person raising the toast is polite behaviour. Like many toasts worldwide, *skol* wishes the recipients good health.

An alternative, and probably untrue, legend holds that *skol* is actually a wish, or exhortation, to Viking allies to persist in battle until they can drink from the skulls of their enemies. That would suggest that Viking weighing *scales* had skulls as the balance pans, a gruesome notion.

Smorgasbord

Smorgasbord is most commonly used in English now to describe something as being a miscellany, a varied medley of items or choices, but that meaning only arose in the 1940s. Earlier use is much more closely tied to eating and food.

The Swedish word *smögåsbord* entered English (and lost the accents present in the Swedish spelling) in the late 1800s. The word translates literally as *butter goose table* thanks to *smör* (butter) plus *gås* (goose) which has the same roots as the English word goose and finally *bord* (table or board). In fact the goose reference is misleading. Goose was the word used for the small pieces of butter which float to the top of cream when it is being churned. They reminded Swedish dairy-maids of fat geese floating on a lake.

Technically a *smörgås* is a slice of buttered bread, perhaps with a topping (more likely to be cheese rather than goose), and the dish is typically an appetiser taken before meals. The term is now used to describe a buffet style meal composed of both hot and cold dishes, including the open sandwiches which originated the idea.

There are terms for such a buffet across many languages, many of which translate as cold table. The Japan the word for a buffet is *baikingu* and translates as Viking so you may see signs for a Viking lunch at your hotel. The term arrived in Japan in 1957 thanks to a restaurant manager from the Imperial Hotel who liked the *smorgasbords* he encountered on a trip to Sweden. *Smorgasbord* was too tricky to say for Japanese speakers so they simply called it Viking instead.

Steak

From a people who lived by the sea and hadn't much land to rear cattle, we get the name for the turf part of surf n' turf – the *steak*.

Steak entered English in the 1400s, so perhaps not with the original Viking invaders and settlers, but it is believed to come from the Old Norse word for roast meat, *steik*, which is related to *steikja* (to roast on a spit) and ultimately to *steig*, an old root word for stick. Basically we get *steak* from a Viking who decided to put some meat on a stick and cook it over a fire. A form of Viking barbecue?

Whisk

Whisk is a late 1300s verb in English for a quick, sweeping movement and it started with cleaning floors rather than making omelettes. *Whisk* comes from the Old Norse word *visk* (a wisp of hay or something to sweep with). It has Proto-Germanic roots and has cousin words in Danish, Dutch, and German to do with brooms and brushes. It wasn't until the 1660s that using a *whisk* to beat eggs came into English usage.

2. Raiders from the Sea

Vikings are perhaps best known for their prowess as sailors. When I researched nautical terms for the first book in this series, "Words The Sea Gave Us", their influence on the development of sailing and navigation was clear. The Viking vocabulary legacy to nautical English is vast.

They certainly weren't the first to take to water, but they innovated in ship design and much of their success from Iceland to Russia and as far south as North Africa depended upon their ability to sail long distances in both shallow and deep waters. Their sturdy ships were light and hence could be moved across land when necessary. They moved via oar as well as sail - making wind less of an issue. They were double-ended, enabling them to change direction quickly, and crucially had a very shallow draft which allowed them to operate in about one metre (three feet) of water. If you can sail in shallow waters you can explore rivers, land on beaches, and are unlikely to be caught on unknown underwater obstacles like sandbanks and rocks. The Viking invention of the *keel* also made them faster, and hence dangerous.

This chapter covers a selection of the most common words they've given nautical English.

Stand on the deck of a ship and a huge number of the things you'll see around you have Norse roots – *boat, bow, dock, harbour, mast*, and *starboard* for a start. They also gave us names for sea creatures large and small from *shrimp* to *narwhal* and even the fearsome legend of the *kraken*. These are explored in the Viking Zoology chapter. Their use of birds in navigation gave us the concept of the *crow's nest* for a ship's lookout.

It's time to step aboard your longship and sail through the cargo of Viking maritime words we use in English.

Bait

Baiting a hook to attract fish may be as old as time but *bait* has moved with the times. It's near impossible to avoid *clickbait* on the Internet and *jail-bait* is a frequently used term too.

Bait dates back to 1300s as an English word. Proto-Germanic had *beita* as a verb meaning to bite and the Old Norse had *beita* as food, or *bait*, in particular for fish. It's not difficult to imagine seafaring Norse fishermen sharing the word with those on English or Norman shores.

Boat

Boat may be a simple term, and one we're all familiar with, but what's the difference between a *boat* and a ship? One answer relates to size. A *boat* is small to mid-sized compared to a ship and has considerably less cargo carrying capacity. Ships are made to carry cargo or passengers whereas a *boat* is the term for a variety of vessels, including those used for recreation, fishing, life-saving, and ferrying people.

Boat is an old addition to English. It entered as *bat*, in Old English, from the Proto-Germanic root word *bait* which is also the source for *batr* in Old Norse and *boot* in Dutch and *Boot* in German. The French word for *boat* is *bateau* and it also comes from Old English and Norse sources, as does the medieval Latin word *batellus*. It appears that the Vikings may have had a hand in giving us the word *boat*, which seems appropriate given their contribution to sailing and navigation in European history.

Bow

The *bow* is the front of the ship where the sides curve in to a point. The word dates to the 1300s and comes from the Old Norse word *bogr* and Middle Low German *boog*, and Middle Dutch *boech* all of which have connection to bending or curved objects.

It pre-dates the use of the word *bow* to indicate bending the body as an indication of respect but it probably didn't give us that usage, they just came from similar sources.

Bridge

The *bridge*, as used in "Star Trek", is the centre of command on a ship and it dates back to the mid 1800s when the *bridge* was a structure stretching across the vessel, very like a *footbridge*, between or in front of paddle wheels on a steam ship. This raised platform became the spot where the captain issued his orders.

The word *bridge* comes from land to sea. *Bridge* originates in old words for beam or log, presumably the original footbridge of walking over a fallen tree to cross a river. The words then move through various German, Dutch, Norse, and Saxon spellings to reach English.

Bulkhead

A *bulkhead* is a vertical partition in the interior of a ship and has been in English since the 1400s. It's a compound word of *bulk* and *head*. The *bulk* was a framework and may come from the Old Norse *bolkr* (beam, rafter, or partition).

A *bulkhead* is designed both to sub-divide space below decks but also to add structure and rigidity to the design. Having *bulkheads* can slow the spread of fire or water but they were often removed if the vessel was used by pirates as they wanted to maximise their storage space for booty.

The doomed passenger liner *The Titanic* had sixteen compartments and was designed to stay afloat even with four of them flooded. Unfortunately the *bulkheads* between the compartments were not tall enough to contain the water that rushed in when she hit the iceberg and she sank in two and half hours.

Crow's Nest

The *crow's nest* is a small platform near the top of a mast where a lookout could perch looking for land or the sails of another ship. Not all *crow's nests* had a railing or enclosure so being the lookout could be a tricky job, particularly in rough seas or high winds. As the rolling of the ship was amplified by the height of the mast any sailor sent to the crow's nest was considered to be on punishment as even experienced sailors would experience severe sea-sickness in that position.

There was always a crow's nest on whaling vessels so the lookout could spot their prey.

The *crow's nest* was invented by the arctic explorer William Scoresby in 1807 when he lashed a barrel into position.

Legend associates the term *crow's nest* with the Vikings who carried crows or ravens on their ships, sometimes in cages lashed to the mast. When visibility was poor or they had need, they would release one of the birds and then follow its course as it would fly straight for the nearest land. If the crow returned it wasn't able to find land.

The same practice was used in British coastal ships in a later era with a cage of crows carried aboard for use when the helm was unsure of their bearing or in foggy weather as all sailors knew the bird would head for land *as straight as the crow flies* thus giving rise to that expression.

The lookout in the *crow's nest* sighted the New World before Christopher Columbus.

Dock

Long before you *docked* your phone for charging or to play music, and even before an accused stood confined before a judge, boats were *docking* for loading cargo or to be repaired.

A *dock* is a ship's birth or any structure upon which a ship may be held. For example a ship needs a *dry dock* if access is needed for hull repairs or painting.

The word *dock* has humble origins with the Scandinavian word for low ground (*dokk* in Norwegian, for example). It's likely the first dock was a simple furrow a grounded vessel made in a mud bank or shoreline. From there it travelled to Middle Dutch and Middle Low German as *docke* and *dokke* and finally in the late 1400s to English.

Dock also works as a verb relating to the shortening of an animal's tale and this also has Viking roots. It entered English as *dok* in the late 1300s from Old English *docca* (muscle) and Old Norse *dokka* (bundle, girl).

The associated idea of removing a part gives us the notion of *docking someone's pay* and dates from the 1800s.

Eddy

Eddy entered English in the 1400s from the Scottish word *ydy* which probably came from the Old Norse word *ida* for whirlpool. As discussed in the entry for *maelstrom* (see the Myths & Sagas chapter) whirlpools come to English from a Viking tale and there's a particularly nasty one in Scottish waters.

Ferry

Ferrying people about is not always a water-based pursuit now, but when it entered English in the early 1400s, it certainly was. The Old English *ferian* verb described carrying or transporting people and goods, particularly over water. It came from Old Norse *ferja* (to pass over) and from Proto-Germanic *farjan*.

Float

To *float* is to rest on the surface of the water and it entered old English word as *flotian* from Old Norse *flota*. There's also Middle Dutch (*vloten*) and Old High German (*flozzan or flössen*) all of whom arise from the idea of flowing.

Floating as a form of drifting was the original meaning but by 1600 there was a more active sense of setting something *afloat* and it wasn't long until it gained financial overtones (1700s) and airborne *floating* (1600s).

It wasn't until the 1900s that we got a drink called a *float* with the addition of ice cream to a soda, where the ice cream *floats* at the top of the tall glass.

Harbour or Harbor

A *harbour* is typically a safe dwelling place for boats and that's where it entered Middle English in the early 1100s as *herberwe*. It has even older roots in *here-beorg* (Saxon*), here-berg* (Anglian), and *herbergi* (Old Norse, lodgings).

The idea of ships have a safe recess in the coastline eventually gave rise to the idea of safe *harbour* for people ashore too. The use of *harbour* as a verb meaning to give shelter to or to protect came about in the 1300s and later gained a more figurative meaning where somebody *harbours* thoughts about something.

Haven

A *haven* is a place of refuge. In nautical terms it's an inlet or small harbour providing shelter for boats. In news reports it appears you can only have the word *haven* if it is preceded by *safe*, but perhaps safety is implied by *haven*?

Old Norse has *höfn* (haven or harbour) and that passed into Old English as *haefen*.

Helm

The *helm* is the mechanism by which a ship is steered, from Old English *helma* with roots in German and Norse, specifically words denoting a handle or a grasp.

The idea of the *helm* being a handle makes a great deal of sense when you consider early ship steering techniques. The *helm* was, before the advent of the ship's wheel, a large handle which turned the rudder in the water, thus influencing the direction of travel. The job of the *helmsman* is to take the *helm* and steer the ship.

The concept of taking the *helm* of a project and steering it to completion has become common ashore.

Keel

The *keel* is the main structural timber of a ship's hull, typically set in the lowest position, running from bow to stern. The keel is key to the construction of the hull. Viking ship-builders invented the keel. Their ships were square-rigged and prone to instability when tacking close to the wind. Adding a keel prevented this, added stability, and increased speed. This, along with the other ship design features I mentioned in the introduction to this chapter, made Viking ships unique at the time. They were faster, and had better range in various seas, than anything else afloat at the time.

Keel entered English in the 1300s probably from a Scandinavian source because it is found in Old Norse *kjölr*, Danish kjøl, and in Swedish *köl*. All three are possibly from a Proto-Germanic word *gwele* which means to swallow.

Keel is sometimes used to describe specific flat bottomed barge-like boats and this is what gets us the expression *"be on an even keel"* to describe stability.

To turn a boat *keel* side up for maintenance (or in capsizing) is what gives us the idea of *keeling over* in a sudden collapse (from the 1800s).

Keelhauling was a cruel nautical punishment used both by pirates and the Royal Navy from the 1500s. The victim was dragged under the ship, while it was at sea, nearly drowning them, and typically ripping their bodies on barnacles, until they died or were near death. The prisoner would be dragged onto deck, allowed to recover their breath, and then the process was repeated. Sometimes one of the larger cannons was fired while the victim was underwater, hence causing pain in their ears and lead weights might be attached to their legs.

Knot

Knot-tying is a vital skill for any sailor and the word has various uses afloat. Rigging a sailing ship requires various *knots*, the bowline being one example, but *knots* are also associated with speed at sea. The *knot* has been the nautical measure of speed since the 1630s thanks to a simple device used in the Age of Sail. A log would be thrown overboard while the ship was under sail, attached to it was a line with *knots* tied at regular distances (1/120 of a mile between each *knot* was standard). The ship's speed was then measured by an hourglass sand timer for a set time (a half minute for example). The number of *knots* payed out on the line, was the speed.

One *knot* became equivalent to one nautical mile so a speed of ten *knots* will cover approximately ten nautical miles in one hour. This is roughly equal to 11.5 miles per hour as a land speed.

Knots of course existed on land before they were used at sea but sailors invented many of the new designs for specific tasks such as mooring boats, and quick-release *knots* for loosening sails.

English appears to have acquired *knot* from *knutr* in Old Norse via German *Knoten*, Dutch *knot*, and finally as *cnotta* in Old English.

Tying the knot is often used as a term for getting married. This perhaps arises from the old tradition of tying together the hands of the couple in a handfasting ceremony. You can read more about handfasting in the Norse Romance chapter.

One final *knot* story is a sailor's yarn that one day a witch was persuaded by a sailor to sell him some wind. Like Odysseus and the bag of wind the Greek god Aeolos, keeper of the winds, gave him, the sailor was presented with a piece of rope with three *knots* in it. She warned him to untie the first for a breeze, the second for a steady wind, and the third only as a last resort.

The sailor went to sea, delighted with his gift. He untied the first and a gentle breeze billowed out his sails. His ship moved, but too slowly for his liking so he loosened the second *knot* and sped away from shore for his destination. After transacting his business there he boarded his ship once more and looked at the final *knot*. It was getting dark and he wanted to return home quickly. The final *knot* would be the solution to his problem.

He untied the final *knot* and unleashed a hurricane that split the sails and sank the ship beneath angry waves.

Mast

The tall poles in the centre of a ship from which the sails are rigged are known as *masts*. Ships may have no *masts* or up to five. On a ship with five *masts* they would be named as follows – the tallest is the *mainmast*, the second tallest is the *foremast*, the third tallest is the *mizzenmast*. After that comes the *jiggermast* and there's no standard name for the fifth but you may find a *spanker mast* on a barque, schooner, or barquentine.

The word *mast* entered Old English as *maest* from a Proto-Germanic source word *mastaz* which also gives us *mastr* in Old Norse, *maste* in Middle Dutch, *mast* in Danish, and *maide* (stick) in Irish.

On a *single-masted* ship the *mast* was the dividing point between the officer and crew quarters which gives us the expression *before the mast* for somebody serving as an ordinary sailor.

Raft

Unlike Captain Jack Sparrow's fictional *raft* to escape his marooning constructed from sea turtles and lashed together with his own hair, most are made of logs lashed together with ropes.

Raft entered English as rafter in the 1300s and only became *raft* in the late 1400s. *Raft* came from a Scandinavian source with Old Norse providing *raptr* as the word for log. It should be noted that *pt* was pronounced as *ft* in that language so it would have sounded more like *raftr*. Sounds like the Vikings wouldn't have approved of Jack's sea turtle plan.

Reef and Reefer

To *reef* sails is to shorten them by partially tying them up. This is done to slow the ship's speed, perhaps when coming in to a harbour, or to prevent a strong wind from putting too much strain on the sails themselves and ultimately on the masts which bear them.

Old Norse has the word *rif* (*reef* of sail) and the Vikings donated that to German (*reff*), Swedish (*ref*), Norwegian (*riv*), Danish (*reb*), as well as *reef* in English by the 1300s. By the 1660s it was being used as a verb to describe the action of taking in or rolling up part of a sail on a ship.

The use of *reef* to describe a coral area in the sea arose in the 1700s and may have been inspired by its long and apparently folded structures (like a folded sail) when viewed by shipboard explorers.

Reefer was first used in a nautical sense. In the 1800s, he was the midshipman responsible for *reefing* in the topsails, so clearly someone with an excellent head for heights. By the 1920s, *reefer* had a new meaning as a marijuana cigarette, or one who smoked them (with a head for highs, rather than heights), thanks to its resemblance to a rolled up sail.

Sheet
{with thanks to Rick Ellrod}

A *sheet* is not a sail, as you might guess from the idea of a bedsheet being an expanse of fabric like a sail. No, a *sheet* is the rope (or sometimes chain) fixed to the lower corners of a sail to keep it in place.

A *sheet* with this meaning, as opposed to bed linen, has been in English since the late 1200s and is a shortening of the Old English *sceatline* (*sheet line*) from *sceata* (lower part of a sail). *Sceata* was originally the word for a piece of cloth. *Sheet* and *sceatlines* are very similar to words in other nearby countries such as *skaut* (Old Norse), *schoot* (Dutch), and *Schote* (German) for the same thing. It's possible this is one the Vikings gave us.

Starboard

Despite early navigation using the stars, the word *starboard* (the right side of the vessel when facing the front) has nothing celestial about it.

Starboard entered Old English as *steorbord* and literally translated as *steer-board* – the side on which a vessel is steering. *Steorbord* came from the word *steor* which was a rudder or steering paddle used to control the boat's direction.

The same concept is found in other Germanic languages of the time - *stjornbordi* in Old Norse, *stürbord* in Low German, and *stuurboord* in Dutch - because all their boats were steered by a paddle on the right side. Similar words in French and Italian are loanwords from the Germanic languages.

The invention of the centreline rudder, brought to Europe by returning crusaders made the *starboard* side steering paddle redundant and now boats can tie up on either the *starboard* or port side.

Stern

The *stern* is the rear of the ship. The word (with this sense, not in the grim and forbidding sense which is entirely different unless you have an unhappy boat) entered English in the early 1200s from the Old Norse word *stjorn* which was a steering paddle set at the back of older ships.

Sunstones

Vikings navigated from the Baltic to Greenland, Iceland, and Newfoundland (which they called Vinland) using sundials. In those northerly seas, overcast and foggy days caused issues for any sundial user.

To circumvent this the Vikings used *sunstones*, rock crystals. Recent research in the Arctic Ocean on the Swedish icebreaker *Oden* proved that *sunstones* such as cordierite, calcite, and tourmaline work like polarising filters and can pinpoint the position of the sun despite cloud cover. Fans of the TV series "Vikings" will have seen this method in action.

This method explains how the great Viking seafarers managed such arduous journeys in an era before accurate charts and time pieces, many centuries before the Age of Exploration led by the Portuguese and Spanish fleets.

Wharf

A *wharf* is a level quay or pier to which a ship may tie up in order to load or unload.

Wharf entered English via the Old English word *hwearf* (shore or bank where ships can tie up) so the meaning was clear from the very beginning. Old English also had *hwearfian* (to turn) from Old Norse *hverfa* (to turn around) so this may be another seafaring term English borrowed from the Vikings.

The idea of a *wharf* rat (1836), somebody who hangs around docks evolved from actual rats (1812) who were common in *wharf* areas and ships (quantities of tasty cargo available were sure to be a factor).

A *wharfinger* arose as an English word in the 1500s in a similar compound structure as *messenger* with roots in *wharfage* (provision or accommodation at wharves) but this time meaning somebody who operates or manages a *wharf*. This term isn't used much now, having been replaced by harbourmaster.

The port city of Antwerp in Belgium is a compound word from *hand* and *wharf* (*werpum* in German).

Windlass

A *windlass* is a form of winch which wraps a rope around a cylinder, especially used on a boat or in a harbour. The winch itself has a land-based origin but the *windlass* has been linked to water throughout history.

Archimedes (died 212 B.C.), the Greek mathematician, inventor, and astronomer, invented the *windlass*. He's also the discoverer of the Archimedes Principle that a body immersed in water displaces an equal volume of water – a discovery popularly believed to have been made when he took a bath, and rejoiced over with the exclamation "Eureka!"

Through history *windlasses* were used to lift heavy masonry in constructing stone buildings but also cocking crossbows, lifting water from wells, opening the lock gates on canals, and as an alternative to the capstan in raising the anchor.

Despite its Greek origins the word *windlass* appears to have Old Norse roots in English. Old Norse has *vindass* from *vind* (to wind) and *ass* (pole or beam). This moved directly to Anglo-French *windas*, then to *wyndase* in the late 1200s and finally as *windlass* in English.

The town of Windsor in Berkshire, England is best known as site of Windsor Castle, a primary residence of the British Royal family. Its name in Old English (1036) was *Windlesoran* which translates as a bank or slope with a *windlass*.

Wreck

A *wreck* is perhaps the most tragic of all types of ship, a broken one.

The word *wreck* started in English in the 1200s as a name for the goods cast ashore after a ship sank and it came to English from the Old Norse *wrek* (flotsam) via Anglo-French *wrec*.

Using *wreck* to indicate a *shipwreck* didn't happen in English until the 1400s and it also took up the verb use then as meaning to take vengeance on something or to destroy or ruin something. By the late 1700s it could also be used to describe a person who had *wrecked* themselves perhaps through wild living.

The idea of a *wrecker* as being somebody who salvaged cargo from wrecked ships arose only in the early 1800s and gained overtones in British English as being somebody who might help cause the *wreck* in the first place, but there's very little historic evidence of such evil work ever being done despite its popular place in legend and fiction.

During the same century *wrecker* was a legal occupation in the Bahamas and the Florida Keys as salvage work.

From the late 1800s it also applied to the work of those who *wrecked* and plundered institutions – something like an early corporate raider, perhaps?

With the advent of motor vehicles the word *wreck* applied to accidents on the roads as well as at sea.

Shipwreck is compounded from *ship* and *wreck* but the earlier word for it in Middle English was *schipbreke* (ship break) from various North Sea languages *skipbrek* (North Frisian), *schipbroke* (Middle Dutch), *Schiffbruch* (German), and *scipgebroc* (Old English). The idea of salvage rights was there from the start as Old English also has *scipbryce* – the right to claim goods from a *wrecked* ship. The debris and cargo from a *wrecked* ship has always been too valuable to simply float away on the tide.

3. Farming

It's often forgotten that not all Vikings were raiders. In fact many Vikings treated raiding as a part-time job. Crops were sown in the spring. During the summer those men and women with a yearning to travel, acquire wealth and battle honour took to their boats while others stayed at home to tend the farms. The raiding parties usually returned home to gather the harvest in the autumn and tell tall tales around the fire during the long dark winter.

Such raiders couldn't help noticing the quality of the land in the countries they encountered and it wasn't long before Vikings were seeking to settle and raise crops in the fertile soil. By the 870s the Danes had traded sword for plow and were settled across most of northern England in an area governed by a series of treaties with the Anglo-Saxons known as the Danelaw.

Hence it's unsurprising that some of the words the Vikings gave us relate to farming life. The words themselves give some idea of what type of farming the Vikings did at home and abroad. They gave us *flock* and *crook* so clearly there was livestock aplenty (you'll find Viking farm animals such as a *ram* and *bull* in the Viking Zoology chapter). Like every farmer they understood the importance of the earth itself so English also acquired *dirt, midden*, and *muck* from them. You might expect *slaughter*, but it's hard to match the mental image of a helmeted Viking, even the farming variety, with *yarn* and *wicker*.

Cart

As long as there have been farms there's been a need to transport goods to market, animals to slaughter, or fodder to livestock which is where the *cart* comes in. The original Old English word for a *cart* was a *craet*, a word with links to words for basket work so the body of the *cart* may have been a woven affair.

Around 1200 the related Old Norse word *kartr* became more popular to describe a typically two-wheeled vehicle usually pulled by a horse and the name stuck around as *cart*.

The phrase *to put the cart before the horse,* to reverse the proper order of things, arose in the 1510s.

Clip

Clip joined English around 1200 to describe cutting with a sharp instrument. It's from a Scandinavian source but which one is unclear as there's a list of them – Old Norse *(klippa)*, Swedish *(klippa)*, and Danish *(klippe)*.

Clipping was used about shearing sheep, but also for cutting small parts off coins (1400 and probably earlier) to cheat people and a known issue for Viking coinage.

To *clip somebody's wings* (to limit them) comes from the method to prevent a captive bird flying away. *Film clips* were literally cut from a reel of celluloid in the pre-digital age. Authors and journalists often keep a *clips file* of their published work much as a visual artist keeps a portfolio. Prohibition in the U.S.A. gave us the *clip-joint*, a place that overcharges.

Crook and Crooked

A *crook*, a hook-shaped tool, is an essential piece of kit for any farmer, especially one who keeps sheep. The word entered English around 1200 from Old Norse *krokr* (*hook*). By the late 1400s it could refer to any bend or curve and often was used for a shepherd's staff with a curved top. That association is what gives us the bishop's *crozier* as his congregation is meant to be his flock (however *crozier* comes from French and Latin rather than Old Norse).

Crook gained an early association with misdeeds as even in Middle English it was associated with the evil tricks of the Devil. By the 1700s, *crooked* was a way to describe dishonest conduct and in 1879 it landed in American English as another word for a swindler.

Crook is also slang in Australia and New Zealand for feeling ill, angry, or upset.

Dirt

Dirt came to English around 1300 and was spelled *drit* originally. It arrived from *drit* in Old Norse and was used to describe loose earth, mud, dung, or foul substances. The more modern spelling of *dirt* didn't arise until the 1400s.

Almost as soon as it arrived it was being used to hurl abuse at people.

Dirt has found its way into many different phrases. *Pay dirt* was miners' slang during the California Gold Rush for the type of soil containing the much sought after gold, *dirt cheap* dates back to the 1700s and *dirt poor* came about in the early 1900s.

Dirty yields a few gems too. *Dirty trick* arrived in the 1600s, *dirty work* in the 1700s, *dirty joke* in the 1800s despite the prudish reputation of Victorian England, and *dirty look* in the 1900s.

Perhaps the most expressive use of *dirty* is the idea of *washing one's dirty linen in public* i.e. to expose private family secrets to the public gaze.

Flock

A *flock* can be a group of animals or people and it was originally spelled as *flocc* in Old English and came from Old Norse *flokkr* for a crowd or troop of people, not animals.

The Old English *flocc* referred to people first and extended to animals moving together only around 1200 and later again (1300) to domesticated animals. The idea of a congregation being a *flock* in a Christian sense arose in the mid 1300s and the application of *flock* to a group of birds only arrived in the 1800s.

Knacker

This noun should be used with caution (or not at all) in English as it has been subverted from its original use into a term of abuse for members of the Travelling Community in Ireland. However it has an honourable history and that's why I'm including it. As a verb it is used to describe someone who is completely exhausted and although it isn't, is regarded as slang in that usage.

Knacker dates from the 1800s in English to describe somebody who slaughters worn out old horses, an important job in a society who relied on horses for transport, power, and agriculture. That task presumably grew from the original job of the *knacker* or *nacker* who was a maker and repairer of harnesses and saddles for horses – a term that dates back to the 1500s at least.

This job, a roving harness mender who would call to farms, fix the tackle, and then move to the next farm, was a highly valued craft and was often done by skilled members of the Travelling community. *Nacker* probably came from Norse roots thanks to *hnakkur* (saddle). *Hnakkur* came from *hnakki* (back of the neck).

Midden

A *midden* is a rubbish heap and is a valuable source for archaeologists worldwide. It's surprising what you can learn about a people from what they leave behind.

The word *midden* dates to the 1300s in English and is of Scandinavian origin. Old Norse had *myki-dyngi* (dungheap) while Danish has *mødding* for the same idea from the word *møg* for muck (see below).

In a pleasant rounding out of the concept, the archaeological use of *midden* to describe a prehistoric place for disposing of kitchen refuse etc. is from Danish excavations in the 1800s so we could claim the first *middens* to be studied in this way were actually made by the Vikings themselves.

Muck

Any good farmer knows their land will only be productive if the soil is nourished and the most common additive available to a farmer is dung. As a result *muck* was important to Viking farmers.

By the mid 1200s the word *muk* (the precursor to *muck* in modern English) had landed in the English dictionary. From the start it was associated with farming. *Muk* was animal or human excrement and vegetable matter spread as manure. It came from Old Norse *myki* or *mykr* (cow dung). It has hung around in Danish too as *møg*.

Root

The underground part of a plant was originally a *rot* in Old English which came from Old Norse *rot* (*root*, cause, origin). The short word replaced older words in English *wyrttruma* and *wyrtwala*, no major loss there I think.

From plants the word *root* spread to refer to teeth and hair in the 1200s, mathematics in the 1500s, and *root beer* (which is made from the extracts of various *roots*) in the 1800s.

The most fun you can have with the word *root* in English is *rootin'-tootin'* which means noisy and boisterous and was first recorded in 1875.

Scythe

A *scythe* isn't a common implement on a modern farm but for centuries, or more, a *scythe* was a farmer's best friend when harvesting crops and cutting hay. It is most associated with images of Death as the grim reaper.

The origin of *scythe* in English is complex. It appears in Old English and Middle English as *sigthe* or *sithe* and is likely to come from the Proto-Germanic word *segitho* (sickle). A *sickle* is a different, much smaller, hand-tool cutting implement you'll see in the hammer and sickle image often used on communist flags.

Some etymologists believe *scythe* reached Old English from *segede* in Middle Low German and *sichte* in Middle Dutch from that Proto-Germanic root word.

Others point at the Old Norse word *sigthr* which is very close in spelling to *sigthe* in Old English. The truth may be a mixture of both theories.

Score

Score entered Late Old English as *scoru* (meaning twenty) from Old Norse *skor* (mark, notch, or rift in rock). It also means twenty in Icelandic, which of course the Vikings also gave us.

The most common use of *score* at the time would have been counting livestock by making a mark on a stick for every batch of twenty. Such tally sticks have been found in the Viking excavations in Dublin, Ireland for example.

Counting in twenties like this is present in languages other than English. For example, any student of French will have despaired of the complexities of counting close to a hundred where ninety eight becomes *quatre-vingt-dix-huit* (four *score*/twenty and ten eight). This specific method of counting even has its own term – *vigesimalism* – and features (or did in the past) in Welsh, Irish, Gaelic, and Breton. Some believe the English and French acquired it from these Celtic languages.

Anybody who thinks we never counted like this in English should cast their mind back to Lincoln's Gettysburg address – "Four *score* and seven years ago".

The *score* could be kept on a stick, marked on a rock, or chalked on a board in the local pub to track your beer bill. By the 1600s this idea was extended to keeping track of the points in a game (*score-keeping*) and by the 1700s other uses had arisen for the word in additional contexts.

First we got *musical scores* (1701) and then *settling scores* (1775) – originally for paying your bar bill and later in a more aggressive vengeful sense. By the 1800s you'd have a *scoreboard* at a match, the *score* for a film arose in the 1920s, *to score* in a sexual sense began in the 1960s (what a surprise), and *scoring* narcotic drugs arose in the 1950s.

Skep

A *skep* isn't a common English word anymore but once nearly every home or farm would have had one, or several. A *skep* is an old-fashioned bee hive. Woven like a basket from twisted straw but then inverted, it provided a home to a small hive.

Skeps are still made today (you'll find instructions online) but are used for transporting summer swarms whereas formerly they were occupied year round.

A *skeppa* was an Icelandic Norse word for a half-bushel grain measure, typically a rounded basket (turn one upside down, add a base, and you have a skep). This travelled to *sceppe*, the Old English word for a basket, and finally gave us *skep*.

The first *skeps* were brought by Saxons to Britain around 400 A.D. and would have come to Ireland shortly thereafter. First official mention of them in Ireland was when Saint Gobhnait in Cork drove off cattle thieves by throwing bee *skeps* at them in 500 A.D. It's unrecorded what the bees thought of that move but I'm assuming the cattle raiders didn't return.

Slaughter

Slaughter became an English word around 1300 and its first meaning related to killing livestock, rather than killing of people which is why it is in the Farming rather than the Fighting chapter.

Slaughter came from Old Norse *slatr* (butchering meat). The idea of a *slaughter* being the killing of many people in battle didn't arise until the mid 1300s. *Slaughter* replaced the Old English word *slieht* (*slaughter*, murder, death).

Smithy

The *smithy* being the workplace of a blacksmith entered English around 1300 from the Old Norse word *smidja*. Any people with Thor and his hammer as a god must have respected such places.

Stack

Stack arrived in English around 1300 from a Scandinavian source to describe a pile or heap of objects. Likely sources include Old Norse *stakkr* (*haystack*), Danish *stak* (also *haystack*), and Swedish *stack* (heap or *stack*). They all have Proto-Germanic roots to a word for a stick so the original *stack* may have been a wood or kindling pile rather than a *haystack*.

In more recent times a *stack* can refer to books (1879), the chimneys of factories and trains (1825), and computer data (1960). *Stacking* is also used as a verb for arranging cards in a deck, piling poker chips, and queuing aircraft waiting to land.

Wicker

Wicker and the idea of *wickerwork* entered English from a Scandinavian source in the mid 1300s (slightly before IKEA). Possibly from Danish *viger* and Middle Swedish *viker* for willow or willow branch, it's ultimately from the Proto-Germanic term *wik* which also gives us *vikja* in Old Norse (move or turn) and *vika* in Swedish (to bend).

Clearly the pliant nature of the willow trees branches had been observed and had proven useful in basket work and woven walls to contain farm animals or to construct dwellings.

Yarn

Yarn is associated almost exclusively with the idea of wool from sheep for the general reader now, although crafters will be aware of *yarn* spun from goat, possum, rabbit, and old t-shirts.

The word root of *yarn* is related to animals but not their fleece. It comes from an old root word *ghere* which means intestine, gut, or entrail. Not sure a sweater made from those would be a good thing. From there, *yarn* wound its way through Dutch, German, and Norse to reach Old English as *gearn* (spun fibre, wool).

4. Norse Romance

It is difficult to know with certainty how romances were conducted in earlier times. The best clues we get are in legal documents. From these historians are able to find clues about how men and women interacted in Anglo Saxon and Viking communities. We know most about the men of the time, but tantalising facts are available about how women lived at the time too and hence, how relationships were made and lived.

In Anglo Saxon life a woman did have some legal rights. She could own property and bequeath it (as shown in wills). She was expected to be virtuous, however, and divorce was extremely rare. Once married she largely had to do as her husband told her. Women were urged not to enjoy romantic relations and were often married in their early teens. One route to independence was to enter a convent. Such establishments, while subject to a male church hierarchy were run by abbesses who often had great power in their locality.

Meanwhile Viking females had more options. Again they married as young as twelve but at least both parties were expected to enjoy intimacy. Dowries were important (explained in the word *gift*, see below). The women ran the farms and households for months, or even years at a time, when the menfolk sailed off in their longships.

Free Viking women could inherit property, request a divorce, and reclaim their dowries if they ended the marriage. There is evidence that the women travelled with the men to settle lands like Iceland and England. If their homes were threatened they would fight alongside the men to protect what they had. Additionally large groups of highly trained female warriors existed. The shield maidens participated in large battles (see more details on the shield maiden life in the Fight Like a Viking chapter).

Perhaps the most telling of female details is that the Anglo Saxon female ideal was Mary, the virginal mother of Jesus, while the Vikings had a range of female goddess to admire plus the female valkyries selecting which warriors had earned entry to Valhalla. It is likely this translated into women being more free to choose who they loved than in Anglo Saxon communities. However often the marriage was arranged between two families to foster links and support for when the winters were long and hard.

There is even some evidence in the sagas that male-male relationships were tolerated in Viking society, so long as the men in question still lay with their wives, something that would have been unthinkable in Anglo Saxon life.

It is unknown how much the example of Viking romance affected Anglo Saxons who lived nearby, but many romantic words edged into the English language during those times. *Enthralling* has a grim backstory but where would English romance be without *hug, kiss, husband, honeymoon*, or *happy*? Perhaps the Saxons picked up a few tips on how to court their women from watching the more enthusiastic Viking partnerships? Certainly the rising popularity of *handfasting* ceremonies in recent years hints at the lasting romantic influence of the Viking way of loving.

Birth

We get the word for *childbirth* and the fact of being born from the Old Norse word *byrdr*. In Middle English *birth* was sometimes even used to describe the conception of a child. The suffix *–th* in this word is to indicate the word is for a process (like death, growth, strength, and even bath).

Bloom

We get this word for the blossom of a plant from the Old Norse *blomi* (flowers, *blooms*). The verb is from the same source. Since 1752 *bloom* can also be used to describe the flush of somebody's cheeks.

Buck

While *buck* in the sense of a male deer comes to English from Old Saxon and Germanic sources, *buck* in the sense of a man took a different path. It entered English around 1300 directly from the Old Norse *bokki* which was used in the same way. It certainly expands the idea of a stag-night for a prospective bridegroom.

By the 1700s a *buck* was a fashionable man about town and we have two common phrases thanks to *buck* and America. *Pass the buck* is 1800s American English slang associated with poker, possibly thanks to a buckhorn knife being used as a counter to pass on your turn in the game. Over time the idea of *passing the buck* came to be seen as avoiding responsibility. By the 1950s *the buck stops here* was famously linked to President Harry Truman (served from 1945 to 1953). He was given a desk sign with the phrase (by an avid poker player) which he proudly displayed in the Oval Office to show that ultimate responsibility rested with him. When

Jimmy Carter took office he arranged to borrow the sign for his own time in office.

Enthrall

Slavery has been a stain on humanity for thousands of years and Vikings were no exceptions.

To *enthrall* somebody, to hold them in bondage, dates to the 1500s in English and is now most used in a romantic sense akin to bewitching somebody. However its word roots are to a more direct form of slavery.

Enthrall is a compound word created from *en* (put in) and *thrall* (slave). A *thrall* is an old word for a slave which comes from the Old English word *prael* (bondman, serf, slave) and ultimately from the Old Norse word *praell* for a slave or servant who had no rights and was treated as being on the same level as cattle.

While Vikings didn't invent slavery, they made a thriving industry from slave trading. They acquired slaves during their voyages and raids on the British Isles and eastern Europe. Certain Vikings laws enabled slavery too. For example, if a woman stole from somebody her punishment might be to become that person's slave. Certain Viking towns became centres for the trading of *thralls* - Hedeby and Dublin, for example. Dursey Island on Ireland's Wild Atlantic Way (which you can visit via cable car from the mainland) was used as a staging post in this trade by the Vikings. They gathered slaves there before export.

Christian authorities of the time particularly objected to the Viking practice of taking Christian people as *thralls*. Dublin's bustling slave market was particularly ironic as

Ireland's Christian patron saint, Patrick, was first brought to Ireland as a slave himself by native Irish traders, centuries before the Vikings landed.

Over time Christian conversions amongst the Vikings reduced the prevalence of slavery. Sometimes slaves could buy their freedom or be granted it by their owners but rules to govern the practice were included in laws from 1241 so this reduction in *enthrallment* took considerable time.

Fellow

Fellow has been an English word for a companion or comrade since 1200 when it arrived as *feolaga* (partner, one who shares with another) from the Old Norse word *felagi. Felagi* was a word compounded from *fe* (money) and *lag* (to lie down). The presumed sense is that a *fellow* is one who puts down money with another in a joint venture.

By the 1300s the idea of money had largely been lost and a *fellow* was one of the same kind or one of a pair (a glove and its *fellow*, for example). Since the mid 1400s it has primarily been associated with males, but originally fellow was used of men or women. Equally variable has been its use in an implied positive or negative sense.

Again by the mid 1400s it was being used to describe a member of an educational college and soon thereafter you might encounter the expression *Hail fellow well met* (on intimate terms). In the 1600s you'd have a *fellow traveller* in the literal sense of somebody you journeyed with but in the 1900s such a phrase referred to somebody who sympathised with the Communist party but wasn't a member.

Bedfellow was somebody you shared a bed with from the 1400s but it is more likely to refer to somebody with similar aims and beliefs in contemporary English.

Perhaps the most amusing *fellow* is the *fellow-countryman*. This expression was held up by British English speakers to mock American English speakers because it is redundant to say both. That was until it was pointed out that it dates to the 1580s and was used by Lord Byron, the famous British romantic poet and politician.

Gift

Gift became an English word in the mid 1200s for that which is given, from Old Norse *gift* (*gift* or good luck). *Gift* was part of surnames from the 1100s. Old English also had *gift* (from similar Proto-Germanic sources) but it was only used for dowries, the idea of a bride-price or marriage gift given by the groom being very important at that time.

Shortly after *gift* arrived in English it gained a second meaning, that of a natural talent or inspiration (perhaps given by God) which leads to the word *gifted*.

Vikings exchanged *gifts* during courtship even though some matches were made more for power and family influence than for love, as was common elsewhere during the era too.

A woman would make her suitor a shirt if she liked him and he might give her purple flowers. During the wedding ceremony the bride would give her groom a new sword. He'd then thrust it into the central pillar of the house and the depth of the cut determined how successful their union would be (the sexual link on that gesture is pretty clear).

The bride typically brought fabric, a spinning wheel, a loom, and a bed to the marriage. Richer women might bring jewellery, animals, and even farms too. Whatever a woman *gifted* to the marriage remained her property (even in widowhood or divorce) and could be left to her children.

The groom also made key *gifts* as part of the marriage. First there was *mundr* – a set price from groom to bride's father essentially to prove he had the means to support a woman and any offspring. Second was the *morgengifu* (*morning gift*) from the husband to the wife the morning after their wedding which she retained in her own right. This could be land, slaves, animals, money etc. depending on the wealth of her husband and gave her much more independence than woman in other societies of the time. Lastly came the *heimanfylgia* – the woman's inheritance from her father which was given to the groom for his use. However in the event of a widowhood or divorce this had to be repaid to the woman for her use.

The idea of a loan also came from the Vikings and is discussed in the Power & Politics chapter.

Generally the meanings of related words in modern Scandinavian languages are similar to Old Norse but *gift* is an exception. It means married in Danish, Norwegian, and Swedish.

Handfast

Viking wedding traditions were numerous and varied. Weddings were typically held during the long summer days and usually on a Friday in honour of Frigg, Odin's wife. Frigg was the goddess of love, marriage, childbirth, and motherhood.

The costumes of the bride and groom might be simple but the bride would wear a special bridal crown which was often a family heirloom and the longer her hair was, the better. Meanwhile the groom might carry a symbolic weapon to finish his outfit.

The couple exchanged swords before rings. Both would be family weapons. Thereafter they exchanged rings, offered on the hilts of the swords.

At the wedding feast the couple had to drink bridal ale (usually a honey-based mead drink) and the marriage wasn't binding legally until they did so. Viking weddings were not sober affairs and lasted for a week.

Handfasting was also part of the ceremony, when the couples' hands were literally tied together with strands of cord or fabric in symbolic colours to show they were now united as one. This type of wedding ceremony was also used in Anglo Saxon times (and well into the 1700s in Scotland). Such a gesture is now making a comeback in modern services thanks, in part at least, to television programmes like "Vikings", "The Last Kingdom", and "Outlander" which all featured *handfastings*.

The verb *handfast* came into English in the early 1100s from Old English *handfaesten* and probably from Old Norse *handfesta*. It is unclear whether the practise came from the Saxons, the Vikings, or indeed from their Germanic tribal ancestors first, but the simplicity and symbolism of the ceremony clearly made it a popular form of wedding ceremony which persisted long into the age of Christianity.

Happy

The most romantic of stories end with the words *and they all lived happily ever after* but did you know that phrase was first recorded in English in 1825? So it's not quite the ancient story-ending we might believe thanks to the bedtime fairytales of our youth.

However *happy*, and *happily*, does date back a bit, to the Vikings again.

The first step to *happily ever after* is to the shorter word *hap* – it means chance, fortune, or fate and it arrived in English around 1200 from the Old Norse word *happ*. There are similar words in several languages, Norwegian for example, has *heppa* (lucky). Old Norse only had a positive sense for *happ*. You couldn't have bad luck and call it *happ*.

Happ gave English *happy* in the 1300s as a way of describing somebody or something as being lucky or fortunate. By the 1500s, *happy* also described being very pleased and content.

Happiness is linked to luck in many languages, from Irish to Greek, during that era. Welsh is one exception – the root for *happiness* there was wisdom.

Old English did have three close cousin words which were replaced by *happy*. The first was *eadig* (wealthy), the second was *geasaelig* which turned into silly, and the last was *blide* which survived into modern English as blithe.

Although, as already mentioned, *happily ever after* arrived in the 1800s the concept of a story having a *happy ending* arose in the 1700s.

Here's one last gem of *happiness* to conclude – the clam. *Happy as a clam* was recorded in English as early as the 1630s. The entire phrase originally talked about being *as a happy as a clam in the mud at high tide* (when it couldn't be dug up and eaten).

Honeymoon

Mead - the *honey*, water, and yeast alcoholic drink popular in Vikings time, in ancient Greece, and thereafter - was an important part of Viking culture. They believed it came about to seal a deal between two sets of warring gods who spat into a bowl to confirm their oath. Yes, they thought mead was divine spit. Warriors arriving in the afterlife in Valhalla would be greeted by beautiful maidens and large mug of mead so clearly it was vital for any good Viking party.

Viking tradition held that a newly wed couple would be provided with a 28 day (lunar cycle) supply of mead – the *honeymoon*. The drink was believed to help the couple in the bedroom department.

Honeymoon (or *hony moone*) arrived in English during the 1500s from that Viking tradition. French has the same idea in *lune de miel* (moon of honey) while German has *flitterwochen* (tinsel week).

Hug

The word *hug* is, sadly, a relatively late addition to the English dictionary. It arrived in the 1560s and was spelled as *hugge*, at least initially. Its origin is technically unknown but it's suggested that it came from the Old Norse word *hugga* which translates beautifully as to comfort.

Hugga itself comes from *hugr* (courage, mood) and is from a Proto-Germanic root which also gives us *hycgan* (to think or consider) in Old English and the name *Hugh*. There may also be a link to the German verb *hegen* (to foster or cherish) which originally meant to enclose with a hedge but while a hedge may enclose, the idea of comforting is closest to what a *hug* means today.

Husband

Until the late 1200s the Old English word for a married man was *wer* but around then it was replaced by *husbonda* to describe the male head of a household, the master of the house.

Husbonda came from the Old Norse word *hūsbōndi*, where *hūs* is house and *bōndi* means holder. At that time only a male could be the main householder. By the 1680s it had been shortened in slang to *hubby*.

Kiss

Kiss entered English as the Old English word *cyssan* and it described touching with the lips but in respect or reverence rather than romantic *kissing*, at least initially. The word itself has Proto-Germanic roots and variants exist across many northern European languages – Old Norse (*kyssa*), Middle Dutch (*cussen*), Norwegian and Danish (*kysse*), and *kyssa* in Swedish.

Phrases including *kissing* often have surprisingly old origins. *Kiss my ass* (or arse) dates from the 1700s but may have been in use in Chaucer's time. *Kiss and tell* comes from the 1600s and *kiss the dust* to describe death is from 1835.

Lass & Lad

A young woman has been a *lass* in English since the early 1300s and it's probably with thanks to the Vikings, or at least their Scandinavian descendants. Old Swedish had *løsk kona* for an unmarried woman, Old Norse had *loskr* for idle or weak (which seems a bit harsh on the *lasses*), and Old Danish had *las* for rag which can sometimes be linked with girl in slang.

Lass and *lad* are often linked in English phrases and *lad* also has Norse roots. *Ladde* was a term for a foot soldier in English since the same period, or for a young male servant, and possibly came from Norwegian terms ending in *ladd* which were compound words for young man.

Meek

Hard though it is to imagine, given shield maidens and the Valkyrie, the word *meek*, especially to describe a woman, came to English from the Vikings.

Meek joined English as *mēk* in the late 1100s with the meaning of gentle-tempered and humble when describing a woman. The basic idea was of female modesty and it came from Old Norse *mjukr* (soft, pliant, gentle) and ultimately from a Proto-Germanic root word that gives us soft in Dutch and humility in Gothic.

The gentle humility of the *meek* changed around a century later to be submissive, obedient, and docile, but that would be a stretch for any Viking woman. The meaning may have been influenced by the more patriarchal Anglo Saxon society.

Seemly

The adjective *seemly* may appear to be a rather Victorian era way to describe somebody of pleasing appearance who is proper and decorous in their behaviour, so it's a surprise to find it in English from the early 1200s and thanks to the Vikings too.

Seemly comes from *semlich* the Old Norse word for honourable or becoming. Old Norse also had *soemleitr* (fine to look at) which may have contributed too.

Ugly
{with thanks to My Name Is Taken on CritiqueCircle}

Although they say love is blind, it can't always ignore ugliness. *Ugly* entered English in the 1200s originally spelled as *uglike* (frightening or horrible in appearance) from Old Norse *uggligr* (dreadful or fearful) which comes from the word *ugga* (to fear).

Thanks to my informant who tells me that in Swedish *uggla* means owl and *rugguggla* means scruffy or describes an owl when it is moulting its feathers. They suggested perhaps that led to the visual image of an *ugly* person.

5. Power & Politics

Considering how Vikings are often portrayed in Old English accounts as being lawless heathens because of their raids on the monks writing the accounts, it may surprise many how often the English language has dipped into Viking vocabulary for the words to describe the structures of justice, politics, and law. We have them to thank for *blackmail* and *gallows* so crime definitely met punishment in Viking society.

The truth, of course, is that while they may have appeared lawless to others, Viking society could never had conquered an area stretching from Greenland to Russia and traded from the Arctic circle to the Middle East without laws, power structures, and rules. In fact the longest running democratic parliament in the world is the Viking one established in Iceland in 930 A.D. (see *thing* below).

Viking society shared many similarities with England in terms of how it managed power. Most worked the land. Farmers (and their slaves) in Denmark lived similar lives to those in England although the land was richer in the British Isles and that attracted Viking settlers.

Above the farmers, certain men gathered power, often through successful raiding and wars. In Viking countries the titles for such men were jarls (*earls*). They were local warlords or chieftains. Later in the Viking era some jarls rose to kingship and the other jarls became nobles much as in England you had a king with nobles beneath him ruling over freemen and slaves.

Women had more power in Viking society than in other communities of the same era. While their primary role was in the home they travelled on the longships with the men to settle new lands, they could own property in their own right, request divorces, and reclaim their dowry if a marriage failed. This was very different from the limited rights assigned to women in Anglo Saxon society. With the Viking menfolk frequently absent for long periods (or killed in battle) the women ran the farm or businesses during those times. Some women also became *shield maidens*, female warriors equal in status to the male fighters.

The words below reflect the effect of Viking political and power structures on the countries they conquered and settled, in particular the developing English nation and its language. Too often when thinking of great European empires we consider only the influence of the Romans on the Europe of today and the English we speak. The Viking influence was significant too and left us with political words like *bylaw, haggle, hustings,* and even *ombudsman.*

Blackmail

Blackmail, the idea of threatening somebody with the exposure of their secrets in return for money is an unpleasant concept and has nothing to do with the idea of *mailing* (American English) or posting (British English) the threat in letter format.

It is, as you might expect, a word compounded from *black* (a comment on *blackmail* being evil) and *mail*. *Blackmail* joined English in the mid 1500s to describe paying criminals fee to prevent pillage. *Mail* in this case came from Middle English *male* (rent or tribute), from Old English *mal* (lawsuit or agreement), and before that from Old Norse *mal* (agreement). Early Viking invaders of England were often paid off to leave, so it's not surprising that they contributed part of the word.

However, the Vikings weren't pillaging in the 1500s, so who were the first *blackmailers*? The term was associated with rogue clan chieftains who exploited farmers in Scotland and northern England and their protection rackets ran until the mid 1700s. By the 1800s *blackmail* had acquired the addition meaning of extortion by threat of scandal, the meaning we are more likely to use today.

There was also, in the 1500s, the idea of *silver mail* (rent paid via coin, rather than trade goods) and *buttock mail* (a Scottish fine for fornication).

Blithering

Today's most common use of the word *blithering* is in the phrase *blithering idiot*, so including it in the political chapter seemed appropriate. Finding its Viking roots takes some patience.

The story starts with *blather*, a verb from the 1500s (spelled as *blether* in Scottish) probably from Old Norse *bladra* (mutter or wag the tongue). *Blathering* was to talk in a nonsensical or foolish way and is still used in Scotland, Ireland, and northern England (classic Viking country in language influence terms).

From *blather* we got *blither* in the 1800s which was also seen as a word from northern Britain and Scotland.

Blithering landed in the late 1800s, formed from the verb *to blither*.

Blithering is particularly handy for shouting at disliked politicians on television debates – "Stop your *blithering*!"

Bluetooth

Bluetooth enables the wireless transfer of photos, documents, and messages. It was developed by the Swedish company Ericsson in 1994.

Harald *Bluetooth* Gormsson was King of Denmark and parts of Norway from 958-987 when he was murdered on the orders of his son. He is most famous for bringing together various Danish tribes into a united nation and even bringing them together with some of their Norwegian neighbours. It was this ability to bring people together that inspired the naming of *bluetooth* technology in his honour. The *bluetooth* symbol is a monogram of the two runes of King Harald's initials.

Historians are not certain how King Harald got his nickname but most guess he had a prominent blackened tooth (the word used in the old texts to describe his tooth as blue has over-tones of black as well as blue).

Bylaw

Bylaw (or *by-law*) comes to English as *bilage* in the late 1200s from either the Old Norse or Old Danish word *bi-lagu*. A *bi-lagu* was a town law – one that applied to local residents in a specific place and this is the sense it retains. The *bi* part in *bi-lagu* comes from *byr* which means a place where people dwell, a town or village and *lagu* simply means law. Even in Viking times local problems and disputes needed local laws and solutions to maintain the peace in their settlements and we still use *bylaws* for that purpose today.

Earl

An *earl* in the British aristocracy is a noble title with roots in Anglo Saxon and a heavy Viking influence. *Earl* in Anglo Saxon translated as a chieftain, particularly one given a territory to rule on behalf of the king. The Vikings had an equivalent term *jarl* at the same time, but this later died out and was replaced with duke. The Scandinavian *jarl* was a petty prince and roughly equivalent to kings in other territories.

In contemporary British nobility an *earl* is below a marquess but above a viscount. The female form is countess.

Earl entered Old English spelled as *eorl* – a warrior chief and contrasting with *ceorl* (churl, and ordinary man). After the Battle of Hastings in 1066 *earl* was adopted as the rough equivalent of count.

Perhaps the most famous *earl* in the dictionary is Charles, the second *Earl* Grey (1764-1845) and a Whig Prime Minister. Legend has it that he provided the original recipe for *Earl* Grey tea – a Chinese blend with bergamot oil when a grateful Chinese mandarin who presented the *earl* with the blend as a thank you because one of Grey's men saved his son from drowning. This colourful story is unlikely to be true. *Earl* Grey never set foot in China and the use of bergamot oil to scent tea was unknown at the time in that country.

Note – the use of both grey and gray are correct in English, although gray is more popular in American

English and grey in British English. As Charles was British, I've chosen Grey.

Gallows

The word *gallows* arrived into written English around 1300 as a plural of the Middle English *galwe*, which in turn came either from Old Norse *galgi* or Old English/ Mercian *galga* or West Saxon *gealga*. As all three of those languages existed on the same small island at the same time it is virtually impossible to know which was the originator and they all have the same root word in Proto-Germanic - *galgon* (pole). It is possible they all arose around the same time in multiple places.

In Old English *gallows* are also used to describe the cross of the crucifixion. *Gallows* are always plural because they are made from two poles.

Gormless

Gormless, that wonderfully descriptive word for somebody lacking basic sense and wit, is one of those words the Vikings gave to English but in a rather convoluted way.

Gormless didn't reach the English dictionary until 1746, thus ruling out a direct borrowing from the Viking raiders in earlier times, yet its roots are solidly embedded in Viking soil.

Gome was an English word from 1200 for understanding and it came from Old Norse *gaumr* (care or heed). *Gome* had *less* added to it to describe somebody lacking in understanding or sense as being *gaumless* or *gawmless*. It's believed that *gaumless* finally led to *gormless*.

Gorm does have another Viking link, however. *King Gorm the Old* ruled Denmark from 936 to his death in 958. He lived to about the age of 60, which was old for the times.

Gorm is perhaps best known for fathering three sons – Toke, Knut, and Harald - and being the last Danish king to rule over a kingdom following the Norse gods. Whereas his son, Harald, who ruled after him as King Harald Bluetooth (mentioned above) moved toward Christianity and united Denmark and Norway. Harald and *Gorm*, were linked via legend to Ragnor Lodbrok and Ivarr the Boneless (whose stories are told in the TV series "Vikings"). King *Gorm* is claimed as ancestor to the current Danish royal family.

Grovel

We have William Shakespeare to thank for the word *grovel*, he created it from *grovelling*. *Grovelling* arrived in Middle English as an adjective or adverb to describe somebody being on their face, prostrate.

Grovelling came from the Old Norse word *grufe* (prone) plus the suffix *–ling* which survives in some other words with a slight spelling change e.g. sidelong and headlong. Old Norse also had *grufla* (to *grovel*) and *grufa* (to cower or crouch down).

One can only assume that Viking raiders and conquerors encountered plenty of *grovelling* from their victims.

Haggle & Hack

Every leader knows the power of a good *haggle*. Making bargains and compromises is a core political skill at every level. *Haggle* gained the meaning of arguing about price around 1600 probably thanks to the idea of chopping away at the final price until an acceptable one was agreed. That's widely assumed because the original meaning of *haggle* was to chop or cut unevenly. A *haggler* was also a term for a clumsy workman.

Haggle arose in that way from the word *hack* (to cut roughly) which dates to the 1200s and Old English and ultimately from Old Norse *höggva* (to hew, cut, or strike).

The idea of being *able to hack it* (able to cope) dates to American English in 1955.

Hustings

Hustings in modern English refer to either election campaigning or a meeting where candidates can address potential voters. It has always been related to politics but the form of a *hustings* has changed over time.

Husting was an Old English word for a meeting, court, or tribunal. The meeting was typically of the men who formed the household of a nobleman or king and the original Anglo Saxon word for such an event was *folc-gemot*.

Old Norse contributed *husting* to Old English from *husding* (council) as a compound of *hus* (house, see also *husband* in the Romance chapter) and *ding* (assembly, see also *thing* later in this chapter).

By the 1500s the plural, *hustings*, had become the norm. The use of the term evolved in the 1700s to be a temporary platform for political speeches probably influenced by the Lord Mayor's *Court of Hustings* in London which was held on a platform in the Guildhall.

By the mid 1800s *hustings* had a more general sense relating to elections and the election process.

The *Court of Hustings* was believed to be the oldest in London and had equal jurisdiction to a county court. Although recommended for abolition in the 1870s the court still exists.

Law

Law was spelled as *lagu* in Old English and was defined as a rule, regulation, or right. It came into the English language from the Old Norse word *lagu* (*laws* plural). *Lagu* wasn't used much in Old English where the alternative word *ae* was more common, however over time it became the dominant word.

Laws govern a wide variety of rules and rights in society and the sciences. For example you have *the laws of physics* since the 1660s, *laying down the law* (in this case biblical *law* pronounced from the pulpit) from the 1750s, and *law and order* have been linked from the late 1700s.

As the systems of politics and the courts grew there were *laws* to cover everything from the *poor laws* (to provide for paupers from the pockets of wealthy landowners), corn *laws*, traffic *laws*, tax *laws*, and many more but it all started with the Vikings, despite being rebuked by the native English as being *lawless*.

Loan

The idea of a *loan* may not be directly linked to politics and power in Viking life but any student of power will suggest that following the money is generally a good place to start in understanding key influences in society.

The original word for a *loan* in English was the Old English term *laen* which translated as gift. However this word didn't survive into English. It was replaced by *loan* in the 1100s to describe something which is given on the promise of future return. *Loans* were non-returnable gifts no longer.

The Old Norse word which gives us *loan* is *lan* and has cousin words, thanks to Proto-Germanic, in Frisian, Dutch, and German all referring to *loans* and fiefdoms.

By the 1500s the idea of a *loan* had been subverted by power to be a contribution to public finances which was meant to be voluntary but often wasn't and which was meant to be repaid but again often wasn't. It would be interesting to discover if lands *loaned* by the Anglo Saxons kingdoms to early Viking settlers were meant to be returned but were actually accepted as permanent gifts. A possible communication and lost-in-translation issue at the root of many conflicts?

By 1900 the world and the English language had acquired the concept of a *loan shark*, one who lends at very high interest rates and has a strict collection policy.

Norman & Normandy

The *Normans* conquered England at the Battle of Hastings in 1066, or so nearly every British and Irish school-child learns in history class. The word has been in English since around 1200 according to the dictionaries, although that battle date suggests it may have arrived a little earlier. But who were the *Normans*?

In many ways the *Normans* were Vikings.

The *Normans* were a race drawn from Frankish and Viking roots. Their name for themselves comes from Old French *Normanz* which is the plural of *Normand* (or *Normant*) which literally translated as *north man*. *Normand* came from a Scandinavian word with the same meaning. In Old French describing a man as a *north man* covered everything from Norse to Norwegian, with a side order of proud, fierce, strong, and possibly deceitful which gives some idea of how the French thought of the Vikings.

In Old English the word for a Norwegian was *Nordman*, very close to *Norman*. It is worth noting that non-Vikings of this period didn't distinguish much between Vikings from Denmark, Norway, or Sweden. They were lumped in together as people from the north.

Who were the Franks then? The Franks lived in Francia, the largest post-Roman barbarian empire in Europe – roughly where modern France and Germany are located. They were originally from Germany and although you might guess French was derived from the Old Frankish language, that's not the case. France and the French language came later.

The *Normans* were originally Vikings who settled around 900 in the northern part of the Frankish kingdom. They founded the duchy of *Normandy*, led by a Viking called Rollo and thereafter conquered parts of Italy, Sicily, England, Wales, Scotland, and Ireland. Rollo, who was variously named as being from Denmark or Norway, first came to history's notice when he besieged Paris in 885-886. He led a fascinating life and is the great-great-great-grandfather of William the Conqueror, the *Norman* who won the Battle of Hastings in 1066 and is an ancestor to the present British royal family – a Viking connection often forgotten.

Thanks to the *Normans*, English took a double dose of Norse influence in the early years of its development.

Ombudsman

Admittedly *ombudsman* only entered English in 1959 and the Vikings had departed before then but the word is from Scandinavia (and has Old Norse roots), something most English speakers don't realise.

Ombudsman is a direct borrowing from Swedish where it translates as a commission man and specifically refers to the office of the *justitieombudsmannen* which investigates complaints of abuses by the state against individuals.

Ombudsman in contemporary Swedish comes from the Old Norse word *ombodsmadr* where an *umbod* is a commission.

Outlaw

Outlaw comes from the Old English word *utlaga*. An *utlaga* was somebody out outside the law and hence unable to access its protections and benefits. *Utlaga* came from the Old Norse word *utlagi* (outlaw) from *utlagr*, the adjective that describes somebody as outlawed or banished.

Banishment outside a settlement was a common punishment in Viking society. It was banishment which drove Erik the Red from Iceland and on to discover Greenland, for example (see the Viking Place Names chapter).

Utlagi was a compound word formed from *ut* (out) and *lagu* (the plurla of *lag*, which means *law*).

It's easy to assume that the resident Saxons would have *outlawed* incoming Vikings for misbehaviour but it appears that the Vikings already had the concept of *outlawing* and banishment in their home lands and brought the term with them to Saxon lands.

Scold

A *scold* was a person of ribald speech and later one who was fond of abusive language and they arrived in English in the mid 1100s. The word was especially used of the females of the species.

Scold comes from the Old Norse word *skald* (a poet). This poetic link is likely to be explained by the Germanic and Celtic tradition of a poet being particularly feared for their ability to mock and satirise their enemies, or indeed the enemies of their patrons and chiefs.

Some Celtic stories even record instances where poetry killed its victims with the intensity of the mockery. Poetry readings were dangerous places in that time period and poets were powerful members of society. In Icelandic law books there was a crime called *skaldskapr* relating to a type of poetry which was libel in verse.

Thing

Thing is a massively useful word in English. It can stand in for almost any noun when the correct word escapes the mind for a moment. It has been joined with other common words to create a range of popular words including *anything, nothing, everything, something, plaything*, and *thingamajig*.

Thing's roots lie in Viking power structures. *Thing* entered Old English spelled as *þing* from Old Norse and the term was initially for a meeting, assembly, or discussion. This political root can be traced in Viking history with ease and spotted in the second half of the word *hustings* (see above).

Iceland's national assembly is called the *Althing*. It's the oldest parliament in the world, having been founded in 930, and it originally met in the *thing fields* outside Reykjavik (see Place Names chapter).

Similarly the *Thing Mote* in Dublin, Ireland was a raised mound near the location of Dublin Castle today, where the Vikings met to agree laws to rule the city during centuries of Norse rule. It stood until the late 1600s.

A *thing* meeting could be attended by all free Viking men, there were no restrictions of status or property. The meetings were regular and organised by a law speaker (who could recite all laws previously agreed) and the local chieftain. Disputes were resolved and laws made so it could be a cross between a parliament and court of law. *Things* could be small local affairs, city level like Dublin, or national like Iceland's *Althing*. *Things* often lasted for a few days and attracted community activities like trade and weddings on the sidelines.

By the time Old English had faded as the people's language, the assembly meaning of *thing* had faded too. A *thing* became something which was discussed at a meeting. By the 1300s it indicated a person who was pitied or a personal possession. By the 1600s English had settled on *thing* to be the word for the object you can't name at the moment and it began to join with other words to provide words for *everything* and *anything* (pun intended).

Thing Mote & Tholsel

As discussed above, a *thing* was a Viking assembly for debate and making laws. The *thing mote* (or *thingmount*), while not a commonly used word today, is too interesting to exclude, especially as it is one of the lasting traces of Viking influence still visible in towns today.

The *thing mote* was a raised mound where the *thing* meeting took place. In Dublin the mound was in the modern-day Suffolk Street area which is on higher ground above the River Liffey. This being Dublin, after the Vikings left there was a pub on the spot called *the Thing Mote*. It's now called O'Donoghue's and I have patronised it in the past, although sadly I didn't spot any Vikings.

The idea of a *mote* being a mound may trigger vague school memories of Norman fortifications - the classic *motte and bailey* setup where you have a castle or fort built on an artificial (or part natural) hill called a *motte* and surrounded by a *bailey* fence or wall. According to the dictionaries that *motte* came to English via the French-speaking Normans and ultimately from Latin with a bit of a Germanic influence, but I can't help recalling that the Normans themselves were Viking in origin (see above) and wondering if *mottes* and *motes* were related?

Tholsel is not a word we get from the Vikings, although it does look like one. Many people believe *tholsel* is of Norse origin, they are often reputed locally to have been built by Vikings, and I believe there is potential for an interesting link between *tholsels* and *thing motes*.

Tholsel is formed from two Old English words - *toll* (tax) and *sele* (hall). There is a *tholsel* still standing in many Irish and British towns. It was the place where you paid your taxes and often is a rather lovely old stone building on a main street.

My nearest *tholsel* is in Drogheda, Co. Louth (currently used as the tourist office) and is on a rise above the River Boyne. There's also a good example in Carlingford where it acted as a town-gate (pay your taxes, or we won't let you in) above the waters of Carlingford Lough, in Kilkenny on High Street above the River Nore, and in Viking-founded Wexford and Waterford. There was a *tholsel* in Dublin too, near Christchurch (uphill from the *thing mote* location) but it was demolished in the 1820s, around the same time as the demise of the *tholsel* in Galway.

The current Drogheda *Tholsel* dates to the late 1700s but records say it replaced an earlier *tholsel* on the same spot so it is difficult to know how long it has existed in some form. While evidence of Viking settlement in the area has been hard to find there are hints in local place names and it's hard to believe the Vikings would have ignored the rich and large River Boyne on their exploration and settlement of Ireland's eastern coastline. My personal theory is that the Vikings were in Drogheda, they had a *thing mote*, and it became the *tholsel* when the Normans arrived in the area in the 1100s.

The *tholsel* in Limerick, near the River Shannon, has changed and moved over time but some historians believe it was built by Danish Vikings around 812 even though records show it being created in the 1440s. There is also a site, nearby, of a *thing mount* for Viking assembly meetings.

It is hard not to see a potential connection between the Viking fondness for having a *thing mote* on high ground above a river to do the business of government and the later *tholsels* in similar positions for similar reasons from Norman times. I would love to see this theory tested but as most *tholsels* are still used today for town councils and town halls I suspect we won't be excavating under them for Viking coins any time soon. This is, I should stress, a theory of mine, and can't be treated as proven history.

If you live in a place settled by Normans or Vikings, check out if you have a local *tholsel*. In Scotland it may be called a *tolbooth* instead. Is it on high ground above a river? Do local people think it was created by Normans or Vikings?

Trust

Trust can be either a noun or a verb and both come from Old Norse. The verb form entered English around 1200 and came from *treysta* (to *trust*, rely upon, make safe). The noun (reliance on integrity and religious faith) arrived at about the same time from *traust* (help, confidence, protection, and support).

Through the 1300s and 1400s the idea of *trust* expanded to that of fidelity, faithfulness, and that on which one relies. By the 1500s it acquired a legal sense as a confidence placed in somebody who holds or uses property *entrusted* to him/her by its legal owner and this leads to the idea of *trust funds* in more recent legal parlance.

6. Viking Zoology

The Vikings were too busy conquering northern Europe and beyond to establish a zoo, but as farmers and explorers they inevitably happened upon a variety of creatures and named them. Those names entered the English language and apply to creatures as tiny as a *bug* and as large as the *kraken*.

When Thomas Edison gave the world the concept of a *bug in the machine* which led to the idea of computer coding *bugs*, few would have recalled its Norse roots. More obvious entries in the Viking zoo include *reindeers, narwhals,* and *walrus* but they named some everyday farm animals too thanks to their farming roots and there's even one, *attercop*, I'd love to see making a comeback in our modern English dictionary.

Grab your binoculars as well as your Viking helmet. Join me on a Viking safari.

Attercop

Attercop may not be a commonly used English word, but it is an interesting one.

An *attercop* is a spider and the only place I've found the word used in mainstream English is when Bilbo Baggins taunts the giant spiders in Mirkwood in "The Hobbit" by J.R.R. Tolkien. Tolkien's writing was heavily influenced by his love of the Icelandic sagas, so it's unsurprising that a Viking-influenced word or two might sneak into his novels.

Attercop (also spelled *ettercap*) is a Scottish dialect word for spider or spiteful person dating to the 1400s at least. The Old English spelling was *atorcoppe* which translated literally as poison-head because *ator* was venom and *copp* meaned summit, round-head, or spider. *Copp* also influenced the formation of *cobweb* as a word.

Interestingly *atta* is the Old Norse word for the number eight. Given that venomous spiders are a minority in the 650 species of spiders found in the United Kingdom, perhaps the first part of *attercop* related to leg numbers rather than poison. Either way, according to Mr. Baggins, calling a spider *attercop* is a terrible insult.

Bat

The flying mammal who inspired Batman evolved slowly in the English dictionary. It's only been spelled as *bat* since the 1500s, the original form was *bakke* in Middle English (from 1300s) which came from a Scandinavian source. The candidates are Old Danish – *nathbakke* (night *bat*), Old Swedish – *natbakka* (night *bat*), or Old Norse – *ledrblaka* (*bat*, or literally leather flapper).

Old English did have a word for the nocturnal creatures, *hreremus*, which roughly translates as rattle-mouse. *Flitter-mouse* was also sometimes used in English (1540s) probably as an imitation or borrowing from German's *fledermaus* (*bat*).

Bat was also sometimes used to denigrate an older woman, with a mild suggestion of witchcraft.

Bitch

Bitch was originally spelled as *bicce* and was used to describe a female dog when it entered Old English. It probably came from the Old Norse word *bikkjuna* which was used for a female dog, fox, or wolf. It is possible the *bikkjuna* originated in the Lapp word *pittja*, but not certain.

By 1400 *bitch* was being used as a negative word to describe a woman.

Bug

Bug as the word for an insect is seen as pure American English by most British English speakers and in some cases reviled as slang, however it isn't. In fact *bug* is a rather old word in the English language, predating any English speaking settlers in North America.

Middle English had the word *bugge* (something frightening or a scarecrow) as early as the late 1300s and it's likely to have come from the Old Norse word *búkr* (a tree insect). The fear association links it to *bogill* (a goblin perhaps inspiring J.K. Rowling's wonderful boggart in the Harry Potter series) in Scottish and *bwg* (goblin) in Welsh and perhaps even linked to the idea of a *bogey* or *bogeyman*.

The common dread of creeping things may well have led to the idea of a *bug* being a small creature. Certainly by the 1600s English speakers were well aware of the perils of the *bedbug*.

The concept of something small causing a large problem persisted in the idea of a *bug in a machine* (1889) which may have been coined by Thomas Edison and persists in the computing world today - beware *bugs* in your code.

Bug as another word for a germ or disease arose in 1919 and *to bug* (to annoy) somebody was possible from 1949.

Bull

A male bovine was a *bule* in English around 1200 and it came from Old Norse *boli* (*bull*) with possible influence from Old English *bula*. The *bull* is an un-castrated male, used for breeding, unlike a bullock or steer. From the 1600s the term *bull* extended to the males of other species such as elephants, alligators, and whales.

The idea of a *bull* stock market arose in the 1700s (*bull* markets are optimistic about future growth, bears are the opposite) and it was around then that the expression "*to take the bull by the horns*" also arrived. Being a *bull in a china shop* arose in 1812 and was the title of a popular song shortly thereafter.

Gelding

A *gelding* is a castrated male horse, mule, or donkey. The operation is usually carried out to produce a more docile animal suitable for working.

Gelding in English comes from the Old Norse word *geldr* (barren, not giving milk). *Gelding* was also used as a word for a eunuch and even as a surname, although it's hard to see how such a family name could be passed down except via adoption.

Kid

Many modern English speakers believe *kid* to be recent American English slang for a child and it would be hard for them to be more wrong.

In fact *kid* joined the English dictionary around 1200 to describe the young offspring of a goat and it came from a Scandinavian source, probably *kid* in Old Norse (young goat). Proto-Germanic provided similar words for the same animal to German, Danish, and Swedish.

Using *kid* to describe a child was slang to begin with, but it was Tudor slang, first recorded in a 1599 play by Philip Massinger called "Old Law".

Thereafter both senses lived side by side.

Kid gloves were made from soft leather (not always from a goat) from the 1600s and the associated phrase of handling something with *kid gloves* (delicate and easily stained so hence the meaning - to handle with care) arose in the 1800s.

At the same time *kid* was used to describe skilful young thieves in the 1800s and *kids' stuff* was something easy in the early 1900s thanks to child-centred vaudeville acts and features in newspapers.

By the late 1800s there's a drinking toast – *here's looking at you* – but it's 1942 before the screenwriters of "Casablanca" and Humphrey Bogart make it famous by adding one word, *kid*. Movie buffs know the screenplay was undergoing rewrites during filming and most believe Bogart improvised the line, which was so good they used it twice.

Kraken

Stories of the *kraken* have long been part of sailor-lore but only in recent times has the giant squid been discovered. Marks left by its suction cups on whales no doubt added spice to the tales.

The *kraken* is most associated with Norway. Norwegian is where it gets its name. *Krake* usually means a pole or post, but sometimes a crooked animal, or in this case a giant tentacled creature capable of snapping boats in two and dragging them to the depths.

Stories of the *kraken* are not confined to Norwegian waters, however. Homer included the Scylla in "The Odyssey" which strongly resembles the *kraken* with size and tentacles. Pliny describes them in his "Natural History" (77A.D.) as being common in the Mediterranean Sea. Some theorists even claim the crew of the *Mary Celeste* were taken by one, although ergot poisoning seems more likely.

So although a Viking language gives us the word, *kraken* were known before the first Scandinavian farmer decided to take a summer boat trip.

The discovery of the Colossal Squid (1981) which is even larger than the giant squid further explains the *kraken* tales, despite the fact that sucker marks found on sperm whales are more likely to come from the whale trying to consume the squid, than the other way round. The *kraken* needs a better publicist.

Narwhal

The *narwhal* is a medium-sized whale living in the Arctic seas around Greenland, Russia, and Canada. The male *narwhal* is easy to spot as it has a large single tusk on its head which is actually a protruding canine tooth. The *narwhal* is hence sometimes called the sea unicorn.

The word reached English during the 1600s from the Danish and Norwegian words *narhval*. *Narhval* came from Old Norse *nahvalr* – a compounding of *na* (corpse) and *hvalr* (whale). The *narwhal* is white which might explain the link to ghostly apparitions.

Vikings, who were astute traders, sold spiral *narwhal* tusks as unicorn horns, probably after European traders (who wouldn't have seen the whale themselves as their explorers hadn't reached the Arctic at that point) made the assumption. Medieval Europeans believed such a horn had magical properties, especially against poisons and melancholy. Such horns were literally worth their weight in gold and the Vikings who bought them from the Inuit and later hunted them, were probably very happy to bolster the stories.

The legends lasted for centuries. Queen Elizabeth I of England received a carved and jewel-encrusted *narwhal* tusk worth about £5 million sterling today and claimed as being from a sea unicorn. It was called the Horn of Windsor.

Inuit legend has it that the *narwhal* was created when a woman was dragged into the sea by the harpoon rope she had tied around her waist. Her long hair braid was transformed into the spiral tusk.

Ram

Ram comes from the Old English noun *ramm* to describe a male sheep or a *battering ram*. *Ram* is also found in

German and Dutch and is probably of Old Norse origin from their word *rammr* meaning strong.

Reindeer

Reindeer entered English around 1400 from Old Norse *hreindyri* which is a compound word from *hreinn* (*reindeer*) and *dyr* (animal). It's a clear case of "so good they named it twice". The words are probably connected to a root term *krei* for horn or head and possibly to Lapp or Finnish further back in time.

Both male and female *reindeer* have horns, with the male's antlers being particularly impressive.

Reindeer are most associated now with Santa Claus but as the original Saint Nicholas (270-342) was a bishop in Turkey, a long way from any *reindeer*, the connection is loose at best. The first reference to Santa Claus and *reindeer* was in a 1821 children's poem published in New York and this was followed by the famous 1823 "Twas the Night Before Christmas" by Clement C. Moore.

Slightly before Moore's Christmas classic, *reindeer* had been introduced to Alaska, along with their skilled Sami herders from Lapland to help Inuit who were starving due to the overfishing of whales. A missionary called Sheldon Jackson initiated the idea and the first *reindeer* arrived in 1898. When the herd flourished a businessman called Carl Lomen spotted the potential for a big market in *reindeer* meat and fur.

Loman worked with Macy's department store to run a Christmas parade featuring Santa in a sleigh pulled by *reindeers* and accompanied by Sami herders in their colourful traditional dress. The parades spread, thanks to fake children's letters begging for them, sent to newspapers by Loman himself.

The connection was forged but Lomen's *Reindeer* Company, which owned a quarter of a million *reindeer*, hit a snag when laws about *reindeer* ownership changed, and he was forced out of business.

As for Rudolph, the most famous of them all? He was invented for a colouring book distributed by Montgomery Ward department stories in 1939.

Shrimp

Shrimp, as the name for a small edible crustacean came to English in the 1300s from the Old Norse word *skreppa* for a thin person. In Danish dialect you also have *skrimpe* for thin cattle. By the end of the 1300s *shrimp* was being used to describe a puny person and by the 1680s further insult could be added by calling them a *shrimplet*.

Walrus

Given that these large sea mammals live from Canada to Greenland and around the Russian and Alaskan coasts it is not that surprising that we get their name from the Vikings as those were all Viking dominated waters.

The word entered the English dictionary in the 1600s as a direct borrowing from Dutch. They had formed walrus from *walvis* (whale) and *ros* (horse) which does make a little sense if you consider the animal they were naming. However Old Norse had beaten them to it with *rosmhvalr* and *rostungr* (both meaning *walrus*). I'll hazard a guess that Viking sailors landing on Greenland in the 980s may have seen the creatures before the Dutch spotted them.

7. Myths & Sagas

Saga itself is a Viking borrowing by English thanks to the long poem stories created to explain Norse history. As with many old stories they combine elements of the fantastic with some history and real people to create an origin legend. The Viking legends haven't penetrated the English story-scape in the same way tales of Troy, Greece, and ancient Rome have, but some of the tales have touched the English dictionary as well as the Marvel comics and movies.

The Norse gods have either given us, or heavily influenced, the naming of *Wednesday, Thursday,* and *Friday* so they are part of everyday life in that way. *Trolls* weren't always cute little dolls with strange hair and the Viking effect has gifted us with *yule* and mistletoe traditions at Christmas.

No discussion of Norse *sagas'* influence on English would be complete without a mention of the renowned fantasy writer J.R.R. Tolkien. Raised by an Icelandic nanny, he devoured the *sagas* at a young age and happily relished their influence on his writing. It is hard to see that the tale of Bilbo Baggins, a dragon, a ring of power, and a quest to overthrow evil in Mordor would be the same without Tolkien's early love for the *sagas*. Astute readers of Tolkien and the Völsunga *saga* notice that both feature an all powerful ring and a sword which must be reforged, for example. There are even similarities between Gandalf (Tolkien's main wizard) and the Viking god Odin.

Friday

Frigg, the Norse goddess of wisdom, is the source for *Friday*. She was Odin's wife and queen of the gods. She could see the future but tragically despite this gift she couldn't prevent the death of her son Baldir, thanks to Loki's trickery, with a mistletoe staff. But afterwards she banished it always to grow high on other trees. This is why we hang mistletoe at Christmas. It must be kept aloft, away from causing harm.

Friday has a different root in Latin. The Romans called it *dies Veneris*, day of Venus, and French speakers will recognise that in their name for the day, *Vendredi*. Venus was a busy goddess. She looked after love, sex, fertility, beauty, victory, and prostitution.

Maelstrom

Maelstrom is used as a synonym for whirlpool and was originally the name for the strong tidal current moving past the Lofoten Islands in Norway, near the Arctic Circle. Various legends surrounded that particular place – either it was the entrance to hell or the mouth of a giant whale waiting to eat entire ships. When the wind and current are in opposing directions it poses a genuine threat to shipping and could sink a ship so Vikings were wise to be wary of the area.

Maelstrom comes from Norwegian compounding of *male* (to grind or churn) and *strøm* (current).

The Norwegian *maelstrom* loaned another legend to the whirlpool at Swilkie off the Scottish coast via Viking settlers and this story explains why seawater is salty.

The King of Denmark owned a magic mill called Grotti which was tended by two strong women Fenia and Menia (Grotti Finnie and Grotti Minnie, witches in the Scottish version of the tale). They turned the millstones to make peace and prosperity but one day they were captured by a Viking who carried them off in his ship along with the mill. He ordered them to grind salt, a valuable product, and this they continued to do until the ship filled with salt and it sank. They continue this task under the waves and that's why the sea is salty and the waves churn above the mill in a *maelstrom*.

The real reason the seas are salty can be explained with science. As water flows down rivers to the sea it picks up minerals from the land over which it passes. When that water evaporates from the seas (as part of the water cycle) the salt it contains is left behind. As time passes the sea water becomes more and more salty.

Saga

A story described as a *saga* today is often a long one, following a family or group over generations and several locations. From the 1800s *saga* meant a long, convoluted story but originally a *saga* was a specific type of story – a tale from Iceland or Norway written down in the Middle Ages. The word is a direct import to English from Old Norse where *saga* was their word for story.

The original *sagas* were primarily stories about the Vikings who settled in Iceland. They were written in Old Norse, often in verse, and are epic in style. The tales about these pagan (and sometimes Christian) heroes are often realistic but they have fantastic and romantic moments too. Some of the *sagas* are based on the author meeting the people involved, while others are believed to be drawn from earlier oral stories.

J.R.R. Tolkien, author of "The Lord of the Rings" and "The Hobbit", drew upon the sagas for inspiration in his fiction. Physical descriptions of Odin in the *sagas* are strikingly similar to his Gandalf, for example.

Thursday

Thursday, as many know, is named for Thor, yes the one with the hammer.

Thor was the Norse god of thunder who made the thunder with his chariot. He-goats pulled it across the sky and presumably it had rattling wheels and bad suspension to create the noise of thunderstorms.

Thor also has an element named for him, thorium, discovered in 1828 by Jons Jakob Berzelius (1779-1848). It is a radioactive metallic element resembling aluminium and is used in electronic equipment and as a source of nuclear power. Perhaps Thor's hammer was nuclear-powered?

Troll

In modern English a *troll* is most associated with the underside of the internet, a place where the malicious can hide behind their invisible location and deliberately stir emotions in others but the original *troll* wasn't a pleasant creature either.

A *troll* is a supernatural being in Scandinavian folklore whose name comes from the Old Norse word *troll* for an inhuman giant, evil spirit, or monster. It may have Proto-Germanic roots around *truzlan*, walking clumsily, but Swedish also has *trolla* (to charm or bewitch) and Old Norse also had *trolldomr* (witchcraft).

Troll was used in the Viking era in the Shetlands and Orkney. There were many forms recorded – *troll-bull* (supernatural being in the form of a bull), *boar-troll*, *troll-maiden*, *troll-wife*, *trollman* (a wizard), and even a *troll-drum* (a musical instrument used in Lapland magical rites).

The *trolls* were originally perceived as an evil race of giants but with time the fear associated with them faded and by the 1800s Danes and Swedes regarded them as imps and dwarfs who lived underground. They were said to lend and borrow from mankind but you had to be wary as they also liked to steal women and children.

Troll later became a verb in English (1400s) for strolling, or even rolling, about. In the late 1500s *trolling* changed to denote fishing with a moving line and that led to the idea of *trolling* involving bait.

By the 1960s *trolling* was slang for cruising for homosexual encounters. By the 1980s or 1990s the sense of an evil creature living in seclusion combined with the idea of baiting someone, to produce the *internet troll*.

Tuesday

This day's name originates with the Old English *Tiwesdaeg* and Old Norse *tysdagr*. It translates as the day of *Tiw* (also known as *Tyr* or *Tiu*). *Tiw* was the Norse/Germanic god of war and the sky.

Latin writers identified *Tiw* with Mars, their Roman god of war, hence the Latin name for the day, *dies martis* or day of Mars. French speakers will recognise *Mardi* in this derivation.

Tiw was right up there with Thor and Odin in the Valhalla days but his stories are less told in modern times.

He was a one-handed god because of his courage. A giant wolf called Fenris was predicted in prophecy to kill Odin, the king of the Norse gods. The gods decided to restrain the wolf while he was still growing but every bond they devised Fenris tore through.

The gods asked the dwarves to create the best leash in the world using magic. They called it *Gleipnir*. It was made from six things; the noise a cat makes walking, the beard of a woman, the roots of a rock, the sinews of a bear, the breath of a fish, and the spittle of a bird.

Not a tasty potion and you'd have to wonder about the Norse women and their shaving habits.

Fenris wouldn't allow the gods to bind him with *Gleipnir* unless one of them stuck their hand into his mouth first. In a challenge with echoes in modern Roman legends of the mouth of truth, *Tiw* stepped up, put his hand in and promptly lost it, to save Odin.

Harry Potter fans will notice a certain similarity in this tale about Fenris the wily Asgardian wolf and Fenrir the werewolf.

Wednesday

Wednesday entered English as *Wodendaeg* or Woden's Day. Woden is also known as Odin, the Norse god of wisdom, culture, and war.

Odin was the god of heroes. If they died in battle the warriors were brought by the valkyries to Valhalla for eternal feasting. Odin surrendered his right eye in order to drink from Mimir's fountain of knowledge. He was believed to have created humans and the universe.

The story goes that he hung himself on the world tree, pierced his side with a spear and hung there for nine days and nights seeking knowledge of the world through special runes.

Yule

Yule isn't a word used often in English but as the calendar creeps around to December you may stumble upon it describing the season as *yuletide* and wonder why. The answer lies with the Vikings.

Yule was originally an Old English word *geol* for Christmas Day or Christmastide. Tide was a synonym for time in the past. In a world with fewer clocks, a sailor waiting for the tide to float their boat was one way to measure time.

Yule, or *geol*, came from the Old Norse pagan festival of *jol* which was seized upon by Christianity and turned into Christmas, in much the same way that early christians appropriated the festival of *Eostre* and associated with it *Easter*. *Eostre* was a pagan fertility goddess whose symbol was a rabbit. You can see the link to the easter bunny easily. *Eostre* was a Germanic goddess and unlikely to have been part of Norse culture.

Yule or *jol* was celebrated in mid January by the Vikings as a feast to drive away the darkness at that time of year. It wasn't associated with any specific Viking god.

After conversion to Christianity the twelve day period from the 25th of December became the feast of the nativity. This gives us the twelve days of Christmas song, as you might expect and the idea of Twelfth Night. That period of Christmas festivity was known as *yule* or *yuletide* until around 1100 when Christmas became the more used term. *Yule* persisted as the name for Christmas in northern areas of England where Danish settlers were more numerous.

Yule lay dormant until the 1800s when it was revived by writers to describe a particularly festive view of how to celebrate an English Christmas. One tradition of *yule* which lingered was the *yule log*, the idea of hauling in a large log to burn in the family hearth during the festivities. The log each year was traditionally lit with a small piece of the previous year's log. As central heating became more popular the *yule log* diminished in popularity but the echo of it persists in the popular log-shaped chocolate Christmas cake.

Traditionally homes were decked with greenery at Christmas time. Holly, ivy, and mistletoe were most common and each has its own story, typically with pagan roots. Mistletoe is part of these decorations thanks to the story of the death of the Norse god Baldir who was killed by a stave of the plant thanks to a trick by Loki. Thereafter it was banished, never to touch the ground again (it grows on the branches of other trees as a parasite). This is why mistletoe is hung from the ceiling, although it doesn't explain the idea of kissing under it.

8. Norse Anatomy

While the Vikings were no more advanced in biology and medicine than other nations of the same period, relying on folk knowledge and herbal remedies, they have left a small legacy to the science of anatomy. Without them we wouldn't have words for *belly, blister, ill, leg, skin,* or *skull*. Latin is largely the language of doctors, but the Vikings gave them a helping hand.

Belly

The word *belly* for stomach has old roots reaching back to Gothic *balgs* (a wine skin), Old Norse *belgr* (bag, bellows) through Anglian and West Saxon to reach Old English as *belg*. All the versions initially referred to a bag, pouch, or even bellows and it was only in the 1100s that it started to be used as a word for the stomach, particularly when associated with gluttony. A swollen stomach appeared to expand like a full bag or air-filled bellows and sometimes *belly* was used to describe somebody who was full of anger in a similar manner.

In the 1800s using the word *belly* was seen as impolite. Stomach, abdomen, and tummy were used instead. As a result the word *belly* was removed from many Bibles printed at that time.

Blister

We picture Vikings making their long journeys by ship but they covered many miles on land too so perhaps it's fitting that *blister* came from them to English. It may have travelled via Old French *blestre* (*blister*, lump, or bump) but it came from a Scandinavian source – probably Old Norse *blastr* (a blowing) or *blaestri* (swelling) both of which are from a root word *bhlei* (to swell).

Calf

Calf in this case refers to the lower leg rather than a young cow. The word entered English in the early 1300s from the Norse word *kalfi*.

Ill

Ill entered English around 1200 as morally wrong, evil, offensive, hurtful, or difficult. *Ill* came from the Old Norse *illr* (evil, bad, hard, or mean).

The association of *ill* with disease and health issues didn't arise until the mid 1400s probably thanks to an Old Norse expression about something evil.

Leg

Leg joined English in the late 1200s from Old Norse *leggr* (a *leg* or bone of the arm or *leg*). It replaced the Old English word *shank* (which gives us the expression *shank's pony*).

As with other key body parts such as hand, eye, and foot, *leg* contributes a number of expressions to the English language.

A leg of a table (chair etc.) arrived in the 1670s, part of trousers which cover the body's *leg* (1570s), and *leg-business* arrived as a word for ballet in the late 1800s.

To *be on your last legs* (1590s), *leg* as a part of a journey or race arose in sailing first (1860s) and moved into other contexts later. *Shake a leg* originally related to dancing (1860s) and then became an exhortation to hurry up (1880s).

Something *has legs* is show business slang from the 1970s meaning a show will keep running.

Skin

Skin first entered English to describe an animal hide (around 1200) rather than human skin and it came from the Old Norse word *skinn* (animal hide or fur). It was applied to the *skin* of fruits and vegetables from the 1300s.

The evocative phrase the *skin of your teeth* for achieving something by the most narrow of margins joined English from a bible translation (Book of Job) in 1550. To *get under somebody's skin* is from late 1800s. *Skin* is jazz slang for a drum since 1927 and *skinheads* entered the language in 1970.

Skull

In Old English the word for the *skull* was *heafod-bolla*, but with the arrival of the Vikings that was replaced by the Old Norse *skalli* (bald head or *skull*) and *skull*. There are related words in Swedish (*skulle*) and Norwegian (*skult*).

Although it would be wonderful if that meant the Vikings gave us *skullduggery*, sadly the experts say that one is from a mingling of Scottish and English.

9. Viking Place Names

It is impossible to live on the east coast of Ireland, as I do, and ignore the Viking place names. The Vikings sailed around Scotland and down the Irish sea and on around the south coast too, naming or founding various coastal or river settlements, many of which are still important towns today.

Starting at the top of the Irish republic with Carlingford we then pass Skerries, Howth with the island Ireland's Eye (or *Irsk Oy* in Norse as I am informed by **Wordfoolery friend and Howth dweller, Brian Lynch**), Dalkey, Leixlip, Wicklow, Arklow, Wexford, and Waterford. If you were sailing along the same coasts today those are the places you would still moor in as harbours.

Wanting to take a wider view and explore beyond Irish place names I found *Copenhagen, Greenland, Guernsey, Iceland, Norway, Orkney, Oslo, Reykjavik, Russia,* and *Shetland.* It's a list that demonstrates the sheer expanse of Norse exploration. It's a far from complete list, but gives a flavour of how the Vikings raided, traded, and settled various countries and ports. If you're anywhere in northern Europe, check the origin of local place names, you may find Viking fingerprints nearer than you expect.

-By

If a place name ends in the suffix *-by* you can assume it has Norse roots. It means village or farm. For example, *Wetherby* (sheep farm), *Selby* (willow farm), and *Grimsby* (*Grímur's farm*). This is particularly particularly prevalent in England.

Copenhagen

The city of *Copenhagen's* name is compounded of *copen* (meaning cheap) and *havn* (haven), something that the *Copenhagen* tourist board probably keeps pretty quiet in its marketing campaigns.

Dale

Perhaps mostly used in poetry now, a *dale* is the level or gently sloping ground between low hills, usually with a river or stream and of course part of the phrase "*up hill and down dale*". *Dale* entered Old English as *dael* from a Germanic source which also gives similar words to Old Saxon, Dutch, Old Norse *dalr*, and German. While *dale* didn't come directly from the Vikings, it is believed that its continued use, especially in northern England and the *Yorkshire Dales* area, is thanks to their strong influence on language in that region.

Geyser

Geyser is the word for a hot spring, fed by geothermal or volcanic activity beneath the earth's surface. It entered English many centuries after the Vikings, in 1780 to be exact, but it's a direct descendent nonetheless. There's one such spring in the valley of Haukadal in Iceland and it's called *Geysir* so when foreign writers were seeking a generic term for all such springs, they picked *geyser*.

Geysir's name translates literally as "the gusher" thanks to the Old Norse verb *geysa* (to gush). The Vikings themselves didn't call hot springs *geysers*. They preferred more practical terms which indicate how they used them when they discovered them in Iceland. They were *hverr* (cauldron) or *laug* (hot bath).

Greenland

Greenland is a direct translation from Old Norse *Groenland*. It was named that by its European discoverer, Erik Thorvaldsson or Erik the Red, in 986 A.D. because he believed it would induce settlers to go there, if the land had a good name. Clearly the power of advertising and naming rights was well known to Viking explorers.

Unfortunately there's more ice in *Greenland* and more green in Iceland. An ice cap currently covers 80% of *Greenland's* territory and human activity is confined mostly to coastal areas.

Erik's nickname probably came from the colour of his hair. He left his homeland of Norway with his family as a young boy when his father was banished for murder. They settled in Iceland and it was from there that Erik sailed to *Greenland* when he in turn was exiled. He spent three years exploring the place and persuaded 25 ships of settlers to come back to *Greenland* from Iceland when his exile was complete. Only 14 ships survived the journey. They created two settlements.

The Vikings were followed by the ancestors of the Inuit who live there today, around 1200 A.D. and while the Viking settlements died out during the Little Ice Age (1500s-1800s), the Inuit stayed, despite Denmark considering the place to be its colony.

Greenland achieved home rule in 1979 but it still part of the kingdom of Denmark. *Greenland* left the European Union in 1985 (it had joined with Denmark in 1973). The language of the country is *Greenlandic* (an Eskimo-Aleut language), but all children also learn Danish and English.

Guernsey

The island of *Guernsey* in the Channel Islands (between mainland Britain and France) was named by the Vikings. The second half of this compound word is *ey*, the Old Norse word for island. The first half may be a variation of the Norse for green or may be drawn from a Viking's first name, such as *Grani*.

From the 1800s the island's name was adopted (along with that of nearby island Jersey) as a name for a knitted sweater, originally worn by sailors. This use is still alive in Australian English in particular.

Guernsey was never formally ruled by the Vikings although it was conquered by the Normans a century earlier than the rest of Britain. In fact the Normans landed there in 933 under the command of William Longsword, the son of Rollo, the first Duke of Normandy – a man who started life as a Viking.

Iceland

Iceland is the most sparsely populated country in Europe, with less than half a million inhabitants. The first permanent settlement on the island was founded by the Norwegian Ingolfr Arnarson in 874, but it was the 1200s before the island was ceded to formal Norwegian rule. By the 1500s, thanks to various treaties, it was ruled by Denmark. *Iceland* gained independence in 1918 and became a republic in 1944. Their parliament is the longest running in the world.

Before the formal settlement by Arnarson and friends, the discovery of *Iceland* was made by a Norwegian called Naddodd and he named it *Snaeland* (snow land) because it was snowing. A later explorer called Folki Vilgerdarson, whose daughter and livestock died en route, spotted icebergs in the fjord and despondently called the place *Iceland*.

As you may recall from geography lessons – *Iceland* has more green areas and less ice than Greenland, whose settler, Erik the Red (see above) had more settler-enticing notions about naming his country.

Norway

Norway entered Middle English as *Nor-weie*, from Old English *Norweg*. The words ultimately came from Old Norse *Norvegr* which translates as the north way, i.e. the way leading to the north presumably because following the Norwegian coast (or land) would bring you north.

Also in Norse there was *suthrvegar* (south way) as a word for Germany and *austrvegr* (east way) for the Baltic lands to the east of Viking territory. They are all very logical names for lands around your home, especially if you've a strong feeling for directions and navigation.

Orkney

The *Orkney* islands lie north of Scotland, south of Iceland, and west of Norway. For centuries they held a central position in the Viking world.

60% of modern day *Orkney* islanders in Scotland are genetically linked to Norway's population but that's not surprising as Vikings ruled *Orkney* and *Shetland* (now in the U.K.) for nearly 700 years. That's three centuries longer than Roman Britain.

Many place names on the islands are from Viking times. *Orkney* comes from Old Norse *Orkney-jar* (Seal Islands) thanks to the Viking word for seal, *orkn*.

Vikings settled *Orkney* in the late 700s and to an extent replaced the local Pictish population. The islands were used as bases to raid into Scotland, England, and Ireland so Vikings didn't have to return to their homelands during the winter. Ownership of the islands was passed between various Viking leaders over time but their control was strong there until at least the 1400s. Viking maritime laws are still observed by the islanders today.

The islands were finally returned to Scotland in 1468 when they formed part of the dowry of the daughter of King Christian I of Denmark upon her marriage to King James III of Scotland.

Oslo

The capital of Norway, is named for an Old Norse word, *os*, for a tidal estuary or river mouth because of *Oslo's* position.

Reykjavik

The capital city of Iceland, as you might expect, was named by the Vikings. Its name translates as Bay of Smoke from Old Norse *reykja* (to smoke or to reek) and *vik* (bay). It was named thanks to the natural geothermal vents and hot springs present in the area. There was a Viking settlement there from the 800s but it didn't become established as a large town until the 1700s.

Russia

Russia entered English in the 1500s from Medieval Latin but spelled as *Russi* and literally translating as "the people of *Russia*". This was drawn from *Rus* which was the native name for a group of Swedish merchants and warriors (i.e. Vikings) who settled around Kiev in the 800s. It is thought that their name for themselves, *Rus*, translated as "men who row". *Rus* was used in Arabic and in Medieval Greek as *Rhos*, so they were well known. The trading links of the *Rus* Vikings extended as far as the Middle East.

Another theory rests on the Old Norse word *Roprslandi* – the land of rowing – and the old name for *Roslagan* where the Finns first encountered Swedes.

The prosperous *Russian* city states were established and ruled by Vikings and their descendants. As the country of *Russia* emerged they called it *Rossiya* in their own language. This appears to be from the Byzantine Greek word for the land, *Rhosia*.

Scarborough

Those living outside the United Kingdom may be most familiar with the town of *Scarborough* in the lyrics of a song about its fair and a variety of herbs. The large seaside Yorkshire town has been an important gateway to north east England for three thousand years and the castle there, built by King Henry II was an important fort during the Middle Ages.

It was named *Scardaborak* by the Vikings, an Old Norse name meaning "fortified place of a man called *Skarthi*". The man in question was *Thorgils Skarthi* (literally *Thorgils Harelip*). *Skarthi* came from Old Norse *skartd* which could also be translated as a notch or a mountain pass so a more literal reading of the name could be gap hill, which would match the geography of the place.

Anglo Saxon fans have also pointed out that it could have come from their language as the hill with the fort. Given its location in northern England, a combination of both influences is highly likely.

Shetland

Shetland is a group of islands north of Scotland, with a population of 22,000 people, whose name comes from Old Norse *Hjaltland* (hilt land), possibly due to the shape of the islands. The first written accounts of the islands are found in the Norse sagas. The islands were inhabited in neolithic times, later by the Picts, and then conquered by the Vikings around 800.

Like Orkney (see above) the islands remained under Viking control for centuries, until they were traded away for a princess' dowry.

Shetland maintains strong links to its Viking heritage. Nearly all place names are Viking, dozens of Norse archaeological sites exist, 60% of *Shetland* males are of western Norwegian descent and the dialect spoken by *Shetlanders* contains many Old Norse words. On Norwegian National Day the island is draped in Norwegian flags despite being an oil-rich part of Great Britain.

On the last Tuesday of January the inhabitants of Lerwick on the *Shetlands* take part in a community celebration of their Viking roots called Up Helly Aa. Run entirely by volunteers this festival takes thousands of islanders the entire year to prepare for one day and night of wildness.

In the evening, thousands of residents from the capital dress in full Viking costume (or something a little more silly) and parade through the streets led by a Jarl. Then they drag a full size Viking galley ship (which took four months to build) to a particular spot where it is burned in the dark of the night. Dramas, songs, and feasting round out the event. Smaller versions of the festival take place throughout the islands.

10. Modern Vikings

Contemporary Scandinavians no longer take to their longships every summer or hoist a shield and axe when going to work (unless they're serving the tourist industry) but the influence of the Viking nations on the English language is still stronger than many would expect. This chapter explores the words English has acquired in more recent times from the descendants of the Vikings who had such a lasting effect on our language.

It's worth nothing two main categories in these words. The first relates to happiness (another Viking word, see the Norse Romance chapter). The Scandinavian nations regularly score the top spots in international surveys of happiness and this has prompted other countries to look to them for lifestyle advice and related words like *hygge* and *lagom*.

The second category is technology and innovation. A cursory glance at developments in this area would suggest all tech words come from America and Silicon Valley but northern European countries have contributed strongly to the industry too and it is reflected in words we often forget have Scandinavian roots such as *celsius, skype, linux*, and *tetra-pak*.

Celsius

The Swedish astronomer Anders *Celsius* (1701-1744) invented the centigrade temperature scale in 1742. The *Celsius* scale, as it was renamed in 1948 in his honour, is used to measure temperatures in all countries except the United States, Bahamas, Belize, Cayman Islands, and Liberia. Its previous name, centigrade, was Latin rooted – *centum* (a hundred) and *gradus* (steps).

The scale is based on the freezing and boiling points for water – 0 degrees for freezing and 100 for boiling. Hence a warm summer day might be 20-35 degrees depending on your location and anything below zero will be literally "freezing outside" as liquid water will transform to solid ice, hail, or snow.

Celsius was best-known for his astronomy work but he was also a noted mathematician and physicist whose father and grandfather had also been renowned scientists. He was the first to notice a relationship between the aurora borealis and the Earth's magnetic field.

Hygge

Hygge is probably the best known gift of a word from Danish to English, certainly in recent times. *Hygge*, in case you missed all the books and articles, is a "quality of cosiness and comfortable conviviality that engenders a feeling of contentment or well-being". It is pronounced hoo-guh.

Hygge is much-lauded as the reason for Danish happiness. Sitting around chatting with the people you love, perhaps by candlelight or having a bike ride and picnic in the park isn't exclusively Danish of course, but it's a pretty decent export. This is one word and concept we're very happy to get from the descendants of the Vikings.

The word itself came to Danish around 1700 from Old Norwegian with the meaning "well-being" and entered English during the 2000s.

IKEA

The *IKEA* catalogue is distributed twice as widely as the bible each year with more than 200 million copies given away.

The *IKEA* name was created from the initials of its founder Ingvar Kamprad, the name of the farm where he grew up Elmtaryd, and the nearest village Agunnaryd. Ingvar was an early entrepreneur, selling matchboxes as a five year old child.

The company is better known for furniture now than matches. It has over 300 stores in nearly 30 countries. They are driven by a desire for good design but also aim to operate ethically with all their cotton from sustainable sources and half their workers, including half their managers, being female.

The Vikings invaded everywhere they could reach and so did *IKEA*, but the furniture giant brought Swedish meatballs along for the ride. Introduced in the 1980s, two million are eaten in *IKEA* stores worldwide every day.

Kindle

A Viking warrior might not be familiar with an electronic reading device but it still has Norse linguistic roots.

Kindle entered English around 1200 spelled as *cundel* (to set fire to) probably either from Old Norse *kynda* (to light a fire), Old Norse *kyndill* (candle), or Swedish *quindla* (*kindle*). A century later *kindle* also had a figurative meaning for igniting passions and emotions.

The name of the reading device was devised by San Francisco designer Michael Cronan around 2005 with a deliberate nod to the original Norse word. He wanted it to reference the influence of books in lighting our minds and making our world brighter.

Lagom

Lagom, like *hygge* (see above), is a recent word borrowing by English. This time the word is borrowed from Swedish, although the term is also used in Norway. It translates as "just the right amount" and is popularly used to describe keeping things in moderation or in balance.

Lagom (pronounced la-gom) is being credited as contributing to Sweden's regular high scores on international happiness and productivity surveys.

Avoiding extremes through *lagom* supports ideas like taking regular work breaks, keeping your To Do List not too short or too long, uncluttered interior styles (think IKEA, another Swedish donation to the English language), balancing your me-time with social time, and generally looking after your well-being.

The idea of *lagom* being the pursuit of "just enough" does have echoes of Goldilocks seeking the perfect bowl of porridge but its origins lie with the Vikings. The word comes from the phrase *laget om* which means "around the team". In Viking times communal horns of mead would be passed around the team and each would sip their own share, in moderation.

Lego

Lego is a proprietary name for the famous Danish play construction brick system and has been part of English since 1934. It comes from the Danish phrase *leg godt* (play well). The company's founder, Ole Kirk Christiansen (1891-1958) didn't realise initially that *lego* also means "I study" or "I put together" in Latin.

Since its invention, more than 600 billion *lego* bricks have been made. Conscious of criticism of plastic, the company now recycles more than 99% of its plastic waste and is seeking plastic-free alternatives to make their parts.

The company, which is still run by Ole's descendants, sells into more than 140 countries, has spawned movies, theme-parks, stores, TV series, video-games, and still inspires children, and adults, to create, imagine, and play every day.

The naming of the brand began with a staff competition in 1934. Ole asked for suggestions and offered a bottle of homemade wine as the prize. The winner was Ole himself.

Linux

This computer operating system, similar to unix but suitable for use on personal computers was originally created by and named for *Linus* Torvalds (born 1969), a Finnish computer programmer.

Rather than copywriting it for financial gain, he made it available for public use on the internet in 1991. He asked other programmers to suggest improvements to him via email. Only 2% of the current version of *linux* was written by Torvalds who was a student at university when he wrote the original version.

Linux could have been named *Freax*, that was the working title for the project he'd chosen. He rejected *Linux* as too egotistical a title but one of the volunteers helping him renamed it without checking first and it stuck.

Tux, a cute little penguin, is the *Linux* mascot because Torvalds was once bitten by a penguin at a zoo in Australia.

Lykke

No sooner had English-speakers discovered *hygge* and *lagom* (see above), than the next Scandinavian lifestyle advice arrived – *lykke*, pronounced loo-ka.

Lykke is the Danish word for happiness. The idea breaks down into six core concepts – sense of community, acknowledging that money (once basic needs are met) isn't that important for happiness, mental and physical health through getting outdoors, freedom to establish a healthy work-life balance, empathy, and kindness.

Sensible advice from the Viking descendants.

Minecraft

Minecraft is a compound English word but it was created by Swedish computer game designer, Markus Persson. The game, released in 2011, has 91 million players active every month and is the best-selling game of all time (as of May 2019). It can be played in survival mode or creative mode and allows users huge freedom to create their own world within the game. It has spawned a large number of social media channels dedicated to parodies and play-by-play videos based in the *Minecraft* world.

Persson has been a controversial figure in the tech world. He transferred creative authority after the game's launch and left his own company after it was bought by Microsoft.

He started programming at the age of seven and is a member of Mensa and despite substantial charitable work he has been heavily criticised for offensive pronouncements on his twitter account.

Nobel Prize

The annual *Nobel Prize* was founded by Alfred Bernhard *Nobel* (1833-1896). He was a Swedish chemist, manufacturer, and philanthropist. He invented dynamite in 1866. He was a pacifist and thought it would form the core of a country's defence and bring peace to the world.

He made a fortune selling dynamite and trading in oil rights, thus enabling his will to fund the annual award in the fields of physics, chemistry, medicine, literature and peace since 1901. In 1969 an additional award in economics was introduced (and fictionally awarded to President Jed Bartlett in "The West Wing").

Alfred spoke five languages fluently by the age of 17 and held 355 patents by the time of his death. Known for his scientific work, he was also a keen poet and playwright.

His father created the first explosive mines for naval warfare for the Tzar of Russia and they were deployed in the Crimean War. While the family lived in Russia, Alfred's father created central heating and their home was the first house in the country to have it installed. Alfred was tutored at home with his siblings and never studied at university. He learned by working with the leading scientists of the day.

Alfred's dynamite soon turned to warfare usage as well as mining. However his writings on the subject of war show that he believed if both sides had devastating weapons then no war would take place – the mutually assured destruction idea. He didn't live to see how incorrect that notion was proven in World War One.

Nobel also has an element named in his honour. *Nobellium*, an artificially created element, was named for him in 1957. The discovering scientists did *not* win the *Nobel* prize for their work. If you're ever in Stockholm, take time to visit the excellent *Nobel Prize* museum.

Nokia

Nokia came to the attention of the world outside Finland when in 1999 they made the 3210. This became one of the most popular mobile phones in the world, and sold more than a hundred million of them in an era when mobile phone usage was only starting to become more widespread.

The company had begun as a paper mill, established in 1865. The name of the company came from the location of the second paper mill, on the banks of the *Nokianvirta* River. The company merged with others and produced goods as various as toilet paper, bicycle tyres, rubber boots, and electronics.

In 1984 they launched one of their first mobile phones, it weighed 5kg. Within three years their phones were down to a mere 800g and they were on their way. By 1998 they were the world's largest manufacturer of mobile phones.

In 2013, after several difficult years of trading, *Nokia* sold their phone business to Microsoft.

Quisling

A *quisling* is a traitor who collaborates with an invading enemy and it's an eponym English has taken from Norwegian.

Vidkun Abraham *Quisling* (1887-1945) was a Norwegian army officer and politician who worked with the Germans during WWII. He served in the Norwegian army and later in the diplomatic service in Russia and the League of Nations.

In 1933, *Quisling* formed the fascist National Union party but never gained a seat in parliament. In 1939 he urged German occupation of Norway. When Hitler invaded Norway in April 1940 *Quisling* became a puppet Minister President.

Under his rule a thousand Jews were sent to concentration camps. He lived in a reinforced 46-room villa on an island near Oslo and had food tasters in case of poisoning attempts on his life.

He was arrested when the Germans surrendered Oslo in May 1945, found guilty of embezzlement, murder, and high treason. He was shot by firing squad in October 1945. His former home is now a Holocaust museum.

Skype

Skype is communication software which allows video calls, text, and audio between mobile phones, tablets, computers, even smartwatches via the internet.

It has more than 600 millions users worldwide and is a true Baltic creation with the founders Niklas Zennström (Sweden) and Janus Friis (Denmark) joining with a trio of Estonians (Ahti Heinla, Priit Kasesalu, and Jann Tallinn) to create the technology. The company has been sold twice, to eBay and Microsoft, in recent years but most of the work is still done in Estonia.

The name *skype* is derived from *sky peer-to-peer* which was shortened to *Skyper* but had to be changed when it was discovered that many of the *skyper* internet domain names were already taken. The team went with *skype* and never looked back.

Stockholm Syndrome

This recognised mental health issue is all to do with power.

Stockholm syndrome is a psychological phenomenon first described in 1973 where those captured or held hostage develop sympathy and other positive feelings towards their captors. It happens in approximately 8% of hostage victims according to FBI statistics.

The syndrome was first identified after a six day bank robbery at Norrmalmstorg, *Stockholm*, Sweden. The hostages became emotionally attached to the robbers, rejected help from the police, and defended their captors after their release.

The Norrmalmstorg robbery was the first criminal event covered live on Swedish television.

One of the men involved in the robbery, Clark Olofsson, had his conviction squashed by the court of appeal. He insisted he'd been trying to keep the hostages safe. He wasn't involved in the initial robbery but did have a long record of similar crimes. After his release he met with one of the hostages many times and their families became friends.

A similar, but reverse, effect is Lima syndrome where the captor develops sympathy for their captive. It was named after an attack on the Japanese embassy in Lima, Peru in 1996. A militant movement took hundreds of people hostage at an embassy party but within a few hours released them owing to developing sympathy for them.

Swede

A *swede* is a large, globe-shaped root vegetable. *Swedes* and turnips come from the same botanical family but *swedes* are bigger, tougher-skinned, yellow-fleshed, come from Scandinavia, and are much hardier than a turnip (a little like the Vikings versus the Anglo-Saxons back in the day). Turnips are smaller and have white flesh.

The *swede* was originally called a *Swedish turnip* until the name was shortened. Turnips are called *neeps* in Scotland (*neeps and tatties*, boiled turnip and potatoes, is a popular dish to serve with haggis). Turnips are called *rutabagas* in France and the USA.

Tetra-pak

Tetra-pak was created by a Swedish company, founded in 1943, and is the largest food packaging company in the world. Its cartons for liquid foods like milk and juice, are particularly famous and are regarded as one of Sweden's most successful inventions of all time. The name comes from the *tetrahedron* shape of the product, first made in 1952.

Volvo

This popular Swedish car brand name was registered in 1915. *Volvo* means "I roll" in Latin thanks to the verb *volvere* (roll) and is related to the *volv* part of the word *revolver* which has a rotating or rolling drum for its bullets. The team creating the name took care to avoid words with R or S in them as they can be hard to pronounce in certain countries and they wanted *volvo* to go worldwide.

11. Fight like a Viking

As discussed already, not all Vikings were fighters. A glance across the words in this chapter, however, will convince you that all of them could fight their corner if necessary, be it with words or weapons.

Both men and women trained to fight and their *shield maidens* were renowned. Their shield walls were legendary too, their fleet virtually impossible to defeat, and they were smart fighters who more than once faked a death, filled the coffin with weapons, and leaped out to battle at a funeral. Although they always stayed close to the water and their ships, they also sometimes moved their ships across land using *skids* to surprise their victims. Vikings were not enemies to take lightly.

Old Norse speakers donated words for *anger* and *die* to English along with *sly, scathe,* and *snub* so perhaps they knew a thing or two about verbal battles as well.

Battling wouldn't be the same without *bash, club, gun, helmet, hit, knife, scare*, or *thrust* – we have the north men, and women, to thank for all of those.

A few fighting words deserve special mention – *berserk* was a unique Viking warrior, the origin of *Viking* itself is disputed but fascinating, *ransacking* was legal in Viking times (and different to its modern meaning). Perhaps the most unusual word in this chapter is *mugging*, which arrived in English via a very rambling route from the Viking word for a drinking vessel.

Sit back, at a safe distance, with a *mug* of your favourite hot beverage and discover how to fight like a Viking.

Anger

Anger, initially as a verb c. 1200 and later as a noun, came to English from the Old Norse word *angr* which meant distress, grief, or sorrow. *Angr* has roots in the Proto-Germanic term *angaz* which also gives us the German word often used in English, *angst*.

In Middle English *anger* also described physical pain as well as emotional irritation.

Old Norse had related concepts of *angr-gapi* (a rash or foolish person), *angr-lauss* (free from care), and *angr-lyndi* (sadness or low spirits) so *angr* could describe a wide range of emotions in the Viking world. What a therapist would make of that is beyond me.

Bash

The verb *bash*, meaning to hit violently, has been in English since the 1600s and is likely to be from Old Norse *basca* (to strike). *Basca* is related to Swedish *basa* (to whip or flog) and Danish *baske* (to beat or strike).

The more figurative sense of *bashing* something being abusing it verbally or in writing didn't arise until 1948. That was around the same time the idea of *having a bash* at something (making an attempt) joined English. Also in 1901 *bash* became slang for a wild party thanks to "*on the bash*" meaning on a drunken spree.

Berserk
{with thanks to Peter Sheehan at Peter Sheehan Studio}

To go *berserk* means to act in a crazy and particularly aggressive way. This was suggested by a Wordfoolery reader who spends his spare time being an extra on the "Vikings" television series, so I assume he goes *berserk* at work.

The word *berserk* entered English in the 19th century as a noun used to describe an ancient Norse warrior who fought with uncontrolled ferocity. They struck down anybody nearby, seemed to be unaffected by fire or iron, and bit their shields. The term *berserker* is also used.

Berserk, which we now use to describe frantic or angry activity, was a direct borrowing from the Norse word *berserkr* which is formed by combining two words – *bjorn* (bear) and *serkr* (coat).

The original *berserkers* were champion warriors, mainly in Icelandic tales, who fought in a trance-like state of anger. They were known for battling without armour. They wore animals skins instead. There were three main codes for this form of northern martial art – bear, boar, and wolf and with the coming of Christianity these became emblems on knights' shields.

The *berserker* warriors may have been part of a bear cult. There are accounts in the sagas of them being laid on bear pelts for their funerals. The bear was one of the animals associated with Odin, the father of the Norse gods, so by wearing it they sought his strength and approval.

Bear warrior symbolism survives to this day in armies. The guards of the Danish and British monarchs, the Queen's Guard and the Royal Life Guards, both wear bearskin caps.

In 1015 Norway outlawed *berserkers* and the same happened in Iceland. By the 12th century *berserker* war-bands had disappeared.

The Lewis Chessmen, ancient Norse chess pieces found on the Isle of Lewis in the Outer Hebrides, Scotland, include *berserkers* biting their shields. *Gnashing* of teeth may have been a Viking warrior habit as the word *gnash* in English (adapted from the Middle English *gnasten* for the same idea) probably originated in Old Norse *gnasta*.

Blunder

Blunder has been an English word since the 1300s meaning to stumble about blindly and it comes from the Old Norse word *blundra* (to shut one's eyes). The association with a *blunder* being a mistake, perhaps caused by blindly rushing into battle for example, arose from the 1700s.

Club

The Vikings are better know for wielding shields, axes, and swords but one weapon name they gave to English is the *club*, around 1200, from the Old Norse word *klubba* (cudgel). Swedish and Danish have similar words too.

From this simple source we now have the *clubs suit* (1560s) in a deck of cards, a group of people with a common interest (1660s), and even the *club sandwich* (1899) which in one story at least, with its multiple layers of bread reminded people of the double decker *club cars* on American trains.

Die

To *die*, to cease to live, is a concept which Old English had words for in abundance. There was *diegan* (although proof for that one is lacking), *steorfan* (to starve), and *wesan dead* (become *dead*). Despite having a word for *dead*, they turned to Old Norse to find one for *dying*.

In the mid 1100s the words *dien* (also spelled *deighen*) entered the English dictionary either from Old Norse *deyja* (to *die*) or Old Danish *døja* (same meaning).

Die appears in many phrases. Sound *dying away* when fading came along in the 1500s while the idea of *dying for something* as a form of yearning arose in the 1700s. *Never say die* arose in the 1800s, possibly first used by sailors. Species extinction is a huge problem in this century so it's interesting to find the phrase *die out* being used for it from the 1860s, at the peak of the Industrial Revolution.

A *die*, as a gaming piece, does not come from the same source. It's older than the Vikings, as dice have been found in Rome's Colosseum and Egyptian tombs.

Dint

A *dint* is typically a small hollow in a surface. Your car might acquire one through a minor accident, for example. It sounds fairly modern but in fact has rather old roots.

A *dint* was originally a blow dealt during a combat. The word came to Old English *dynte* or *dynt* from the Old Norse word *dyntr* (stroke, blow, or kick). Subsequently the idea of a *dint* became associated with the mark such a blow might leave on armour. There's also the associated phrase (dating to the 1300s) *by dint of* (by force of, by means of).

Gang

Gang in English came jointly from Old English *gang* (a journey – think of a ship's *gangway* or *gang-plank* for example) and Old Norse *gangr* (a group of men). Both words have the same Proto-Germanic root and are unrelated to the verb to go.

By the mid 1300s the meaning of the word *gang* was evolving from both sources so a *gang* was a set of objects taken together when you're going somewhere. For example, a craftsman might gather his *gang* of tools when setting out to make a repair to a house. By the early 1600s a *gang* was a group of workmen, often in a nautical sense and by the 1630s that *gang* was sometimes spoken of disapprovingly as being rowdy or troublesome, such as a *gang of thieves*.

The badly behaved *gang* idea persisted into the 1800s. Also, American English in the 1700s might refer to a group of slaves working on a plantation as a *gang*.

Gear

Gear, despite sounding modern, has been part of English since 1200 when it was used to describe fighting equipment and weapons. *Gear* probably came from Old Norse *gørvi* (whose plural is *gørvar*).

The Norse word described apparel and *gear* and the idea of being prepared, skilled, and ready to go – attributes which were useful for any raiding party. The underlying verb was used regularly in Old Norse to describe everything from dressing meat to telling a story, it wasn't exclusive to the idea of battle. Its roots in Proto-Germanic produced related words with similar meanings about preparedness and clothing in German, Dutch, and Saxon.

From the early 1300s *gear* began to change meaning. First it referred to clothing and to tackle for horses. Then generally as tools for a specific task, and later for sailing ship rigging tasks in particular. By the 1500s a *gear* was a toothed wheel in a mechanical device and by the 1800s that *gear* was specific to a vehicle like an early car or bicycle.

In the 1950s *gear* gained slang use in Britain (possibly thanks to The Beatles) for something being stylish or excellent and later in the 1900s it returned, again in slang use, to be a set of tools and equipment again, but this time for heroin use.

Gun

Although Vikings preferred axes, swords, and shields as their weapons they gave English the word *gun*. In fact *gun* comes from a female Viking which seems appropriate as Viking shield maidens were fierce female warriors at a time when other countries wanted their women to stay at home and avoid battles.

Gun entered English, spelled as *gunne*, in the 1300s for a machine which propelled rocks, arrows, or other projectiles from a tube thanks to the force of explosive powder and it was a shortening of the female name

Gunilda and is mentioned in an inventory of the armaments at Windsor Castle in 1330.

Gunilda was a borrowing from the Old Norse name *Gunnhildr* which was formed from *gunnr* and *hildr* both of which mean war or battle, so clearly *Gunnhildr* wasn't the meek and mild type. The *gun* was the first of many weapons named for women – the massive Big Bertha *gun* built by Germany during World War I is one notable example and fighter pilots like to give their airplanes female names and cartoons too.

One famous *Gunnhildr* may have created the link to weapons and battles but despite many references in various Viking sagas, historical proof of her existence has thus far been lacking.

The legends claim *Gunnhildr* was the wife of Eric Bloodaxe, the second king of Norway who ruled during the 10th century. She is described as a vicious and outrageous woman from Denmark who may have practiced witchcraft. She was daughter to King Gorm the Old (see *gormless* in the Power & Politics chapter) and sister to King Harald Bluetooth (see *bluetooth* in the Power & Politics chapter). She provided six sons for the family line and when her husband died in battle she led his forces to plunder the British Isles before returning to Denmark where years later she was drowned in a bog by Harald Bluetooth as punishment for plotting treason.

Helmet

Helmet comes from the Old English word *helm* with roots in German, Norse, and various cousins in Saxon and Gothic. Viking *helmets* weren't horned by the way. We have Wagner's costume designer to thank for that.

Hit

Hit comes to modern English from the Late Old English verb *hyttan* (come upon, meet with, *hit upon*) which in turn comes from Old Norse *hitta* (to light upon or strike). There's also Swedish *hitta* (to find) and Danish and Norwegian both have *hitte* (to *hit* or to find).

During the Old English period the meaning shifted from "to come upon" to striking and displaced the verb *slean* (to slay) in the process. However the original meaning persists in the slang *hit on* (1970s) and *hit it off* (1780s) and also as simply *hit it* in the 1630s.

Several phrases include this verb. A *hit song*, book, or movie (1811 onwards) comes from the idea of *hitting a target* (1400s onwards). A *narcotic hit* dates from the 1950s. An ordered killing being a *hit* dates from the 1970s.

Hitting the bottle (1933) is predated by *hit the pipe* from the late 1800s but referring to opium in that case. *Hitting the nail on the head* is one of the oldest and comes from archery in the 1500s. *Hitting the hay* for a sleep isn't as old as you might think, dating only to the early 1900s and *hitting the road* is older than expected (1873). Alternatively you could *hit the bricks* (1909) which was trade union slang for going out on strike.

Knife

Yes, the Scandinavians coined this word too. The *knife*, from Old Norse *knífr* was an important part of Viking culture, and was often buried together with its owner. *Knives* were used for hunting and combat. The modern Swedish word is *kniv*.

Knife was originally *cnif* in late Old English and came from *knifr* which was a *knife* or dirk from the Proto-Germanic root word *knibaz* which yielded similar words in Dutch and German too.

Mug & Mugging

A *mug* of tea is about as English as you can get but while the tea came from India and other nations, the *mug* came from Scandinavia.

Mug entered English in the 1500s as a small cylindrical drinking vessel, often with a handle, from a Scandinavian source. Candidate origin words include – Swedish *mugg* and Norwegian *mugge*.

English potters created popular *mugs* shaped like the faces of people during the 1600s and this led to the idea of a *mug* being a person's face.

With the advent of photography, and particularly the use of it in police work, the idea of a *mug shot* being a photograph used to identify a criminal arose. This idea led into boxing slang where *to mug* was to hit the face of an opponent and this in turn gave us the term *mugging* for an assault on a person with the intent of robbery.

Mug and *muggy* do not have the same roots despite similar spelling. You can read about the origin of *muggy* weather in the Norse Landscape chapter.

Rambo

The famous fighting character played by Sylvester Stallone in several movies wasn't a Viking, but his name does have a surprising connection to Scandinavia, and the Vikings would have liked his tough attitude and fighting ambition.

John James *Rambo* was created by David Morrell in his novel "First Blood" in 1972. Morrell borrowed the character's surname from a variety of apples called *rambo* which he found in Pennsylvania, because he thought they sounded forceful.

The apples were named for Peter Gunnarson *Rambo* (1611-1698) who is also known as the Father of New Sweden. Peter sailed to the New World at the age of 23 in 1639. He worked as a tobacco planter for the New Sweden Trading Company's plantation in an area which is now part of Philadelphia. He adopted the surname *Rambo* around 1640, married, and lived through many key events in the settlement such as its takeover by the Dutch and later the British. He became a member of the governor's council, met William Penn (founder of Pennsylvania), and was the longest surviving of the original Swedish settlers.

Some experts say *Rambo* translates as raven's nest and is related to Ramberget (Raven Mountain) near Gothenburg in Sweden. Peter Gunnarson *Rambo* may have been thinking of home when he chose his new name.

Ransack

Ransack entered English during the 1200s from Old Norse *rannsaka* (to pillage). The word in Norse had a precise meaning – to search a house, legally, to uncover stolen goods, whereas in English it has illegal associations. *Rannsaka* was formed by compounding two words *rann* (house) and *saka* (to search). *Saka* is related to the Old Norse verb *soekja* (to seek).

It's likely the English understanding of the word as being a violent, illegal, raiding of a place came about because of the word *sack* (to plunder). *Sack*, however, didn't have Viking roots.

Sack comes from the Middle French expression *mettre à sac* (put it in a bag) which was a military command to troops, allowing them to plunder a city. The particular idea reaches back through word history to Italian (*sacco*) and Roman armies (*saccus*). In this case the Viking association with *ransack* is legal and calm, and we can blame the Romans for the inspiration for wild plundering.

Scare

There's no doubt the notion of invading Vikings is a *scary* one. One early reader of this book suggested that the main set of words the Vikings gave us was "Help, run away!" so it's unsurprising to find *scare* has Viking roots.

The spelling of *scare* we are familiar with today came about in the 1590s but in Middle English you would have found *skerren* (around 1200) from the Old Norse verb *skirra* (to frighten or shrink from). *Skirra* was related to *skjarr* to describe somebody being timid and afraid. You'd also find similar words like *skair* and *skar* in Scottish and *skeer* in English dialects.

The *scary* carved prows of Viking ships with their intricate curved animals and monsters were detachable and might have been carried before their warriors in an early form *of scare tactics* to inspire fear in those opposing them. *Scare tactics*, as a phrase, entered English in 1948.

Scathe

Scathe is most used in modern English in adapted forms *scathing* and *unscathed*.

Scathe arrived in English around 1200 from Old Norse *skada* (to hurt, injure, damage). *Scathing* was originally a physical injury to an enemy but over time the idea of *scathing* became more associated with verbal damage and by the 1800s this was the most common use of the word, to indicate the hurt caused by invective, sarcasm, and satire.

Shield Maiden

Shield maiden in English does not have Old Norse roots, however we definitely owe the Vikings for the entire concept and a chapter about fighting like a Viking cannot skim over the fact that many of their warriors were female.

Shield entered Old English as *scield* (*shield*) from *skelduz*, the word for a board in Proto-Germanic (which also gives *skjöldr* to Old Norse). It's easy to see how a *shield* was originally any plank of wood used to protect yourself in combat.

Maiden entered Old English as *maegden* (an unmarried woman, usually young), again from Proto-Germanic roots. Put the two together and you have a *shield maiden*, a young woman who wields a *shield*, but *shield maidens* did much more than that.

In Old Norse they used the word *skjaldmaer* and it describes a female warrior. In strict historic terms there's no clear proof of the existence of *shield maidens* but it is commonly accepted for two good reasons. 1) archeological sites containing female remains interred with weapons and armour originally assumed to be male skeletons but now shown to be female and 2) extensive references to *shield maidens* in the Norse sagas.

The sagas were passed via the oral tradition for centuries before being written down so they are not contemporary reports, and do have the odd flourish or two as you'd expect, but increasingly these tales are being proven to be based in fact.

Some of the female warriors mentioned in the sagas include; Brunhilda (known for her honour and dedication to duty), Hervör (a story about a cursed sword), and Lagertha (a warrior and leader whose history was written in the 1100s).

Shield maidens could be any age, married or single, and are reported to have taken part in the very effective Viking combat ploy called the *shield wall.* Women and men fighting together was not an unusual sight in Viking battles. Some *shield maidens* fought in one campaign and then returned to a more domestic role, while others pursued the calling for life. This lifestyle and the history of Lagertha will be familiar to any viewer of the "Vikings" TV series.

JRR Tolkien, who had a huge love for the Norse sagas, named the females of the Rohan people in his books as *shield maidens* (although he depicts them fighting only very rarely) and Peter Jackson's movie of "The Lord of the Rings" shows them living in Viking style clothing and housing.

Skid

Skid is most often used as a verb nowadays and is definitely something you need to avoid when driving on icy roads, but it entered English as a noun around 1600. A *skid* is a beam or plank on which something rests, especially relating to moving something heavy from one location to another.

In the late 1800s in the forests of the American west *skids* were laid down to form a rough road which could be used for hauling out logs without too much friction. These rough lumber tracks were called *skid-roads* and give us *skid row*, more about that below. Viewers of the "Vikings" TV series will have seen a large group of Vikings moving their ships across land using *skids* when they were attacking Paris. Historical accounts tell us they did move ships overland, but it was after the siege, not before.

Skid's origin is likely to be from Old Norse *skid* (a stick of wood or long snow-shoe). This also gives us the word *ski*, as explained in the Daily Life chapter.

Since Viking times, *skid* has given us a few other terms and phrases. By 1890 *skid* had acquired the meaning of sliding along and this transferred to cars from 1903 and in 1914 we got skid-mark as a result. *Skidding* was associated with something going downhill (another possible link to downhill *skiing* perhaps?) so by 1909 you have *hit the skids* for something or somebody going into a rapid decline.

With time *skid roads* in the forest gave rise to the *skid rows* in the local towns, specifically the part of town where the loggers lived. By 1920 *skid row* was describing the area of town where unemployed men would gather (an early reference was to part of Seattle, Washington) and it became a term for a disreputable area, possibly thanks to the idea of lives going downhill and *hitting the skids*.

Sleight

Sleight is best known now in the phrase *sleight of hand* to describe the prestidigitation used in magic tricks and pick-pocketing. The phrase dates to the 1300s but the word first entered English in the 1100s with a different spelling, *sleahthe*, to denote skills, cleverness, and cunning

It came from the Old Norse word *sloegd* with the same meaning, and *sloegr* (sly). It's difficult to picture a stereotypical Viking warrior engaging in subtle *sleights of hand*, but they were known for clever battle stratagems, so perhaps card tricks were in their toolbox too.

Sling

Swords, axes, and shields were the most common Viking weapons but they must have used *slings* to hurl missiles because that's how the word reached the English language. *Sling* entered English around 1200 from the Old Norse word *slyngva*. Later it was associated with tying up a hammock (1690s) and supporting an injured arm (1720).

Sly

Sly has been an adjective in English since 1200 for those who are skilful, clever, and dextrous. It comes from Old Norse *sloegr* (cunning, crafty, sly) from a Proto-Germanic base word with the idea of being able to hit.

Related words in other Germanic languages all have the idea of quick and ready to strike so *sly* wasn't always a mental thing, but rather the ability to strike swiftly at your enemies.

Snare

A *snare* is a noose or trap for catching animals, or figuratively to trap enemies of any type. The word entered late Old English from Old Norse *snara* (noose or snare) which came from *soenri* (twisted rope). It was used figuratively as early as 1300.

Snub

Fighting like a Viking doesn't always involve shields and axes. It can be more subtle. One example is the verb *snub*.

To *snub* somebody is to rebuke or reprove them verbally and it came to English in the 1300s from Old Norse *snubba* (to curse, chide, *snub*, or reprove). The idea came from cutting somebody off in speech and hence is possibly related to the Swedish word *snobba* (to lop off or to snuff out a candle). Old Norse also had *snubbotr* (snubbed, with the tip cut off). The same idea applies to the *snub nose* which is shorter than normal.

The idea in English of *snubbing* meaning to treat somebody coldly in a social context came about in the early 1700s.

Sprint

Sprint only entered English in the 1500s but its source is Old Norse. It's likely to be an altered spelling drawn from *sprenten* (to leap or spring) in the early 1300s. The original Norse source was *spretta* (to jump up) and it also gave Swedish the word *spritta* (to startle). The idea of *sprinting* being to run a short distance at top speed didn't arise until the 1800s.

Thrust

The verb *thrust* entered English in the late 1100s from Old Norse *prysta* (to *thrust*, force, or press).

Thwart

Thwart entered English around 1200 from Old Norse *pvert* (across) as an adjective, possibly from its use in ship-building terminology where a *thwart* is a piece of timber placed crosswise in a boat to brace it and sometimes used as a seat by a rower. By the mid 1200s thwart was also being used as a verb meaning to oppose, hinder, or cross a person.

Viking

If there was ever a word we could guarantee came from the *Vikings* it would have to be the word *Viking*. The word comes from the Old Norse *vīkingr*. Unfortunately *Viking* is the *Viking* word with the most murky history in terms of language.

Viking is a latecomer to English, arriving around 1820 and was often used as a synonym for pirate. It wasn't used in Middle English. In Anglo Saxon chronicles during the *Viking* Age the Norse raiders and soldiers were called *pa Deniscan* (the Danes), regardless of their country of origin. The *Vikings* who settled in England and Scotland were named after the place where they settled.

Several theories exist as to the language origin of the word *Viking*. Here are a selection, you may choose the one you prefer.

First - the Old Norse word *Vikingr* (pirate, *Viking*) means one who came from the fjords because *vik* means inlet or bay in Swedish (but not in Danish or Norwegian and the Danes were the main group of Vikings to land in England).

Second – the Old Norse word *Viking* (freebooting voyage or piracy) comes from the phrase *fara í víking* (to go on a sea expedition) from the Old Norse word *vika* (sea mile). The idea is that *Viking* was a sea expedition and a *Vikingr* was somebody who went on such a voyage.

Third – *Viking* came from *Vikingr* which meant "king of the bays", because they used bays to hide in and then dart out to attack passing ships. This particular one is unlikely. The king connection has never been proven, *Vikings* were more likely to follow earls/jarls rather than kings in the early years, and their method of attack wasn't to hide and pounce from bays.

Fourth – Old English had the word *wicing* and Old Frisian had *wizing* for about 300 years before the first known use of *Viking*r in Old Norse. Those older words were for a village or camp. The *Viking* raiders, when they arrived often established large temporary camps during their visits and the locals may have named them after their locations.

Personally I find the second explanation the most plausible but until some proof is uncovered in a *Viking* saga or other Old Norse/Old English source, the language jury is out on this particular word.

12. Daily Life

When researching Viking words in English it soon became apparent that the vast majority related to simple everyday tasks, actions, emotions, and objects. Siphoning off words for farming tasks, anatomy, and food into their own chapters helped my task but be warned this is still a long chapter.

It wasn't that Anglo Saxon lacked words for many of these things, but over time the Viking word won the battle for use and edged out the native English word. Many would be helpful for small spaces in a crossword or a game of Scrabble – *big, ball, gap, bag, rug, wag, gab,* and *rag*.

Basic verbs abound, words so everyday that we never think of them as overseas imports – *burn, call, cast, crawl, drag, get, gush, hurry, lift, race, raise, scrub, skip, stagger, take*. Others sound a little older – *bolster, dappled, irk, knell, tatter, thrift, thrive,* and *tiding* – but are still used often in modern English, perhaps in ways unimagined by Norse settlers.

What I love about the words in this chapter is the glimpse they offer into a Viking and Anglo Saxon world not so very different from our own. *They* can feel like the *awkward odd* one out, enjoy a *cosy* night at home *knitting* with toes on the *rug*, scan the *sales* for a new *suede skirt*, look out a *window*, relish the *sleuthing* in a crime novel, and plan a *ski* holiday.

The daily life of Vikings which is revealed in this chapter is more recognisable to a modern reader than you might expect.

Awkward

Awkward entered English in the 1300s with a different meaning to the one we understand today. It meant in the wrong direction. So if you'd driven your cart the wrong way to market you would have been doing so *awkwardly*.

By the 1500s this meaning had been replaced by the idea of something or somebody being clumsy, and by the 1700s it could also mean you were embarrassed.

All of this sprang from the root word *awk* (back-handed or turned the wrong way) which was a borrowing from Old Norse *afugr* with the same meaning. *Awk* was a standalone word in English for many centuries but became obsolete in the 1700s. There has been a resurgence of *awk* in the recent slang phrase *totes awks* which is a shortening of *totally awkward*.

Bag

A *bag* as a small sack was given to English as *bagge* around 1200 probably from the Old Norse word *baggi* (pack or bundle).

For an everyday item it has accumulated relatively few related phrase. Letting the *cat out of the bag* (1760) originally related to selling something hidden to conceal its quality (similar to buying *a pig in a poke* as a poke was a pocket or bag) rather than the escaping of secrets and it may have been an adaption of the French phrase *acheter chat en poche* (buy a cat in a *bag*).

After that you had to avoid being left *holding the bag* (the empty bag after being swindled of course, 1793), you could *bag game* or another prize (1814), and if something was *your bag* then it was your kind of thing (1964).

Ball

Ball came to English around 1200 either from an unrecorded Old English word like *beal* which language experts presume existed or from the Old Norse *bollr* (*ball*).

The earliest use of *ball* in the English language was about a *ball* in a game but the associated meanings about the *ball of the foot* and round missiles in warfare arrived around 1400 and the comparison to a testicle was pretty early too.

Ball features in several popular phrases, most of which originated in particular *ball games* – *be on the ball* (1912), *keep your eye on the ball* (1907, probably golf), and the *ball is in somebody else's court* (1960s, tennis).

A *ball* as an organised dance came from French roots – Old French *baller* (to dance).

Big

Old English used the word *micel* (related to much) to indicate that something or somebody was powerful or strong but around 1300 the word *big* creeped into the language, at first mostly in northern England and the midlands (settled Viking strongholds). The source was probably Scandinavian and similar words persist in modern Norwegian, for example.

A short and simple word, it caught on fast and gained additional usage through the following century or two – of large size, fully grown, important, influential.

Big's use in expressions is widespread. The 1800s gave us *big-headed*, *big top* in a circus, and *big game hunting*. The 1900s provided the *big band* musical style, *big business*, *big house* as American slang for prison, and *big ticket items*.

Bleak

Bleak joined English as *bleik* (pale) around 1300 from the Old Norse word *bleikr* (pale, whitish, blonde). *Bleak* meaning pale is long gone but since the 1500s it has mean bare and windswept.

Bolster

A *bolster* is an old word for a pillow. It's typically a longer, and sometimes cylindrical pillow, often used to support other pillows. This leads to the other meaning of the word, a supporting structure. You might be more familiar with the idea of somebody *bolstering* support for their position, perhaps in the political realm. That idea came later, around the mid 1400s.

Bolster entered Old English as a stuffed cushion from Old Norse *bolstr*. There are similar words in Danish, Swedish, Dutch, and German. It's safe to assume that although Vikings could manage tough conditions at sea or in battle, they liked a little comfort in their bed at home.

Burn

Burn joined English as a verb in the 1100s, originally spelled as *brennen* and it covered everything from cooking words like broil or roast, through to *burning* with light, and burning with desire. *Brennen* came to the language from the Old Norse word *brenna* (to burn or light). Irish readers please note - the surname Brennan does not come from this source.

The most common use of the word in Old English was for passion or battles but later it was more associated with the idea of fire and heat.

The common slang now around *burning* or roasting somebody with words is actually much older than you might think as *burning* meaning to cheat, swindle or victimise somebody dates to the 1600s.

The idea of money *burning a hole in your pocket* because it wants to be spent arose in the 1850s and Mark Twain was an early user, or possibly first user, of the phrase *burn your bridges* in 1892 – a concept which has been linked to reckless actions of cavalry in the American Civil War but was surely a military tactic long before that conflict. The military practice of *burning your boats* to prevent retreat goes back at least as far as Roman times, for example.

Call

The verb for crying out, summoning, asking, and naming came to English in the mid 1200s from the Old Norse *kalla*. Earlier in Old English you might have used *ceallian* (to shout) or *clipian*.

Calling has a wide variety of uses in English since its Viking days. *To call for something* in a demanding way dates to the 1500s as does *to call something back* (revoke). The early 1600s gave us *to call somebody names*.

The explosion of *calling* terms occurred in the 1800s. We got *to call the result* of a coin toss, *to call somebody's hand* at cards, *to call something off*, *to call out* somebody to fight, and to make a *telephone call*.

All we got in the 1900s was *to call it a night* and a Christmas song. Although the song is probably older (1700s), the lyrics we sing today date to the 1900s.

The well known Christmas song "The Twelve Days of Christmas" features *four calling birds* but in this case they have little to do with *calling*. Earlier versions of the lyrics presented the receiver with four canary birds or four mockingbirds or ever four *colly* (or *collie*) birds which is an archaic term for blackbirds. *Calling bird* may simply be a handy word to replace *colly* but in case you're still curious, *a calling bird* is a decoy bird which makes a *call* to attract others for hunting purposes.

Cast

The verb to *cast* (1200) entered English from Old Norse *kasta* (to throw) which has related words in Swedish and Danish. It replaced the Old English verb *weorpan* and has nearly been wiped out in its turn by the verb to throw although we still *cast* fishing lines and glances.

Cast had a variety of uses in the language. Originally it could emit (light for example), throw to the ground, throw off something, or find a course on a chart of map. By the end of the 1300s you might also *cast* an astrological calculation to create somebody's horoscope. By the 1500s you could *cast up* to compute your bill, create something using a mould, or even vomit.

By the 1700s *casting* was a way of giving out the parts to the actors in a play and in the 1840s the idea of *casting a vote* arose in American English.

Cosy

This Viking word came to English via Scotland. Anybody living in the northern parts of Europe, be that Viking housewives or Scottish crofters knew the value of being warm and snug in winter so it's no surprise that *cosy* (or *cozy*) entered English from those regions. *Cosy* was originally spelled *colsie* when it arrived in English around 1700. It was a Scottish dialect word with Scandinavian roots – a related expression is the Norwegian *kose seg* (*be cosy*).

To complete a *cosy* afternoon in English all you have to do is add the *tea cosy* to keep your teapot (and its contents) warm – those were created around 1850, probably not by Vikings.

Another recent *cosy* addition is the idea of a *cosy mystery* (or *cozies*) – detective fiction which downplays sex and violence in favour of detection skills in a small setting, the opposite of hard-boiled crime fiction.

Crawl

Crawl entered the English dictionary around 1200 but spelled as *creulen* (to move slowly by dragging your body across the ground) from either Old Norse *krafla* (to claw one's way) or Danish *kravle*.

The idea of a *pub crawl*, perhaps involving dragging yourself between taverns as the night progresses and more alcohol is quaffed, has been known in English since 1883 but there's a chance the Vikings knew about that one too, given their love of mead.

The *crawl* as a swimming stroke was developed in the early 1900s by Frederik Cavill, an English swimmer who emigrated to Australia and was inspired to adjust the standard swim-stoke of the day by watching islanders in the South Seas. It was named the *crawl* because it looks like a swimmer is *crawling* through the water.

Dappled

Dappled, meaning spotted or marked in different shades, entered English in the early 1400s probably from a Scandinavian source drawing on the Old Norse word *depill* which means spot or the Norwegian word *dape* which means splash of water.

A related word is the Old Norse adjective *apalgar* (dapple grey) used to describe the markings on the skin of an apple.

Drag

The Old Norse word *dragga* gives us both noun and verb forms of the word *drag* in English.

Dragging the bottom of a body of water with hooks or to haul something along has been around English since the late 1300s and since the 1660s has given us the idea of moving slowly, *dragging your feet* along the path, although the actual expression about *dragging one's feet* may date from the 1940s and a lazy way to use a saw in the logging industry.

A drag is sometimes better known as a *dragnet* and has been used since the 1700s, at least, as an object to slow things down, for example slowing a returning rocket-ship from space.

Drag in the sense of a man performing while wearing women's clothing joined English from theatre slang in the 1870s perhaps as a reference to the *skirts dragging* along the floor, but the idea of *a drag queen* didn't join the dictionary until the 1940s.

The origin of the phrase *drag racing* is a little more complex. *Drag* was slang for an automobile in the 1930s, possibly from the idea of a wagon being *dragged* by a horse in earlier times or because a main street was often called a *drag* (1850s onwards, primarily in American English). As *drag races* needed a long street, this may be the true origin of the phrase.

Eiderdown

As you snuggle under a feather-filled eiderdown bed covering, spare a thought for the Vikings in their chilly northern homes who named both the *eider duck* and the *eiderdown*.

The name of the *eider duck* reached English in the 1700s from German or Dutch who both had the same word, and both came from an original Old Norse word - *aepar*.

The *eider duck* has warm soft feathers, which it often uses to line its nest and by the late 1700s English had also acquired the word *eiderdown* to describe a bed covering which is filled with these feathers to give warmth through the winter months. Vikings may not have invented the first *eiderdown*, but *eider ducks* live throughout northern Europe and Iceland and the word *eiderdown* originates in Icelandic as *aedardun* and is also found in Danish as *ederdunn* and German as *Eiderdon*.

Gab, Gabble, and Gift of the Gab

To *gab* is a verb meaning to talk a great deal. Its most common usage in modern English is in the phrase *"the gift of the gab"* whose origins are lost in time but whose meaning is clear – to be able to speak articulately and convincingly. The opposite, *to gabble*, is to speak inarticulately and too fast.

One of *gab's* earliest usages in English literature was in the Nun's Priest's Tale in "The Canterbury Tales" by Chaucer which was published around 1400. "I *gabbe* not, so have I joy or bliss" is one line in the story which is read as "I'm not lying with this story because I want to go to heaven."

Hence *gab*, or *gabbe* in the old spelling, means to lie and having the *gift of the gab* actually means you're a skilled liar.

This original association of *gab* with liar came into English from Norse. *Gabber* in Middle English was a liar and *gabben* meant to mock somebody or to lie. It came from Old Norse *gabba* (to mock) and also from Old French *gaber* (to mock or boast) which also came from Scandinavian sources.

By the 1700s *gabbe* had changed to *gab* and the lying had changed to talking too much, and perhaps foolishly.

Gable

The triangular *gable* end of a house's roof is surprisingly similar to the wooden posts (often carved) used to pitch a Viking's tent. By the mid 1300s *gable* had joined English to describe the end of a ridged roof from Old French *gable* and from Old Norse *gafl*. In northern England the word probably skipped French altogether and came direct from Norse.

Both sources had roots in *gablaz*, a Proto-Germanic word for a pitched roof which yielded related words from Dutch to Gothic. *Gablaz* had links to words for forked branches and pitchforks both of which visually resemble the two crossed timbers used to form the edge of the roof, or the timbers at the entrance to a Viking's tent.

Gap & Gape

Gap, meaning a break in a wall or hedge, has been in English since the 1300s. It's a direct borrowing from Old Norse *gap* (empty space).

Gape, to stare open-mouthed, is a related word from the Old Norse *gapa* (to *gape* or open the mouth wide). The original root word is *ghieh* and refers to yawning so perhaps the *gap* in a hedge or a mountain pass was seen to resemble an open mouth stretched in a yawn.

Get

The verb to *get* has been part of English since around 1200 and it comes from the Old Norse verb *geta* which had a variety of meanings from to reach or obtain, right through to the sense of producing offspring.

Almost as soon as it arrived in English, *get* was used in phrases such as *geta rett* (to guess right). It was commonly compounded to make new verbs such as *beget* or *forget.*

The joining of *get* with other words continues to modern times and space prevents a full listing here, but here are a selection of *gets* to *get you started.*

- *Get drunk* 1600s
- *Get religion* 1700s
- *Get out of hand* 1700s
- *Get better* 1700s
- *Get ready* 1800s
- *Get busy* 1900s
- *Get lost 1947* (as in – please go away!)
- *Get on somebody's nerves* 1970

Gloss

While a *gloss* as a comment on a text comes from Latin, the idea of *gloss* being a shiny finish in a photograph or in painting comes to us from the Vikings.

The smooth sheen of *gloss* first appeared in English in the 1500s and probably came from Old Norse *glossi* or the Icelandic word *glossi* for a spark or flame (from the verb *glossa,* to flame), from similar Germanic roots as the English word *glow.*

Gloss is also dialect slang in Scotland for blushing.

Gush

Gush entered English around 1400. The verb describes anything rushing out forcefully, particularly liquids like water or blood. It comes from the Old Norse verb *gusa* (to gush or spurt) and is related to the noun *geyser* (see Place Names chapter). The idea of gushing being a manner of speaking in an effusive manner didn't arise until the late 1800s.

Gust

A *gust* of wind is believed to be a survival word from Old Norse *gustr* – a cold blast of wind, something they would have experienced in their travels.

Hurry

The verb *hurry* is first recorded in the works of William Shakespeare who used it often. It probably came from the Middle English word *hurren* (to buzz quickly like an insect) which came from Old Swedish *hurra* (to whirl around).

A similar set of roots are suggested for *hurtle* and *hurl*.

Irk

To *irk* somebody or be *irksome* is to disturb or annoy and it's been in English since the early 1300s, probably because annoying people (and annoying tasks) have always been with us.

Irken was the original spelling in English and the meaning evolved over time too. Its previous meanings include – to be weary of, to be disgusted with, to be displeased, to be slow or unwilling to do something.

The origin of *irk* isn't certain but the best guess is that it came from Old Norse *yrka* (to work). Anybody who has ever grumbled about going to work can certainly empathise with a Viking link between work and being *irked*.

Knell

Knell is either the act of ringing a bell (spelled *cnyllan* in Old English) or the sound that bell makes (Old English *cnyll*)

It probably came to English from the Old Norse term *knylla* (to beat). There are similar words in Dutch, German, Swedish, Welsh, and Danish.

Knell is often associated with the idea of a death bell (*cnull* in Welsh), tolled to announce a death. Ask not for whom the bell tolls...

Knit

The Old English word for *knitting* was *cnyttan* (to tie with a knot, to bind together) and it was strongly related to the Old Norse word *knytja* (same meaning) and other words in German thanks to their common Proto-Germanic origins.

The idea of *knitting* being a way to create fabric using knots created on two needles didn't arise in language until the 1520s but is likely to pre-date that time as weaving and *knitting* were (and still are) key methods to clothe people when animals skins weren't available or suitable.

Crochet became a craft much later than *knitting* and its name comes from French but *crochet* is the diminutive form of *croc* (hook) which in turn came from Old Norse *krokr* (hook) which is further explained in the entry for *crook* in the Farming chapter. You'll also find *yarn* in that chapter too.

Lift

Lift joined English from the Old Norse verb *lypta* (to raise – note *pt* was pronounced like *ft*). It was used to describe elevating somebody in rank or to pick up from the surface and set upright, like *raise* which is discussed later in this chapter. Middle English also had a twin word *lift* to describe the air or sky above from the Old English word *luft* (air) which gives us the idea of something being *aloft*.

To *give somebody a lift* to cheer them up arose in the 1400s, shortly followed by *lifting* in the *shop-lifting* or thieving sense. *Giving somebody a lift in your vehicle* pre-dates cars considerably having arrived in 1712, while *a lift* being a form of elevator to move people and goods between floors of a building arrived in the 1850s. Perhaps the most recent evolution of the word is the *face lift* which was first mentioned in 1921.

Loose

Loose is one of those words where Old English dithered about the spelling for a while. Standardised spelling of words is relatively recent in fact, but don't try that excuse on your next spelling test.

We had *lous, loos, lowse* and finally *loose* to define something as being unbound or not confined and it came from Old Norse *lauss* (*loose*, free).

Loose arrived in the early 1200s but by the 1400s the meaning had expanded to bring in other ideas. You might have *loose clothes* or a *loose person* could be free of obligations and at liberty. A *loose* person might also be one who was free from moral constraints and hence immoral and unchaste.

Phrases with *loose* in them are equally varied. *A loose end*, either on board ship or in the family loom, was a string or rope indicating an unfinished task. To *be at a loose end*, however, is to be without a task to do, free as a bird and it dates to 1807. *Hang loose,* as an instruction to relax and not take life so seriously, joined in around 1968.

Mistake

Mistake is one of those words where the Viking word blended with pre-existing Anglo Saxon terms for the same thing so seamlessly that it's tough to unravel them afterwards.

It arrived in English in the late 1300s as a mixture between Old Norse *mistaka* (to take in error) and the compounding of *mis* (bad or wrong) and the verb *to take* to produce a term for taking in error and misunderstandings.

Mistakes being an error in opinion or judgement arose in the 1500s.

Oaf

English words can have crazy spelling histories. The standard spellings so beloved by English teachers today are relatively recent creations and *oaf* is a perfect example of this.

Oaf has been an English word and spelled that way since the 1630s, but when it arrived in the 1620s it was *auf* or *oph*. It has a fairytale source (according to some older lexicographers anyhow) because an *oaf* was a changeling, a foolish child left by the fairies in place of the human child they stole away. The word came from either Old Norse *elf* or Norwegian *alfr* (silly person) and led to the idea of an *oaf* being an idiot.

The link to elves is clearer in older dictionaries which claimed the plural of *oaf* wasn't *oafs* but *oaves*. However, it might be best not to use *oaves* in your English essays unless you want your English teacher to faint.

Odd

The adjective *odd* joined English around 1300 from Old Norse *oddi* (third or extra number). The Vikings used the concept frequently. They had an *oddr-madr* - the third man or *odd* man who was able to give the casting vote and the *odda-tala* the *odd* number.

The literal translation of *oddi* related to an angle in a triangle and contributed to words for weapons, often with triangular blades or arrow tips.

The association of *odd* with being strange or unusual didn't arise until the 1500s and began with the idea of being the *odd one out* or the unpaired one in a group of three so it still had its roots in counting and numbers.

Poke

Poke, the verb, hasn't got Viking roots, but *poke* the noun does. A *poke* is an old word for a small sack that dates to the 1200s in English and came from the Old Norse word *poki* (bag, pouch) via Old French.

Poke isn't used often in modern English writing but you may have seen references to a poke of tobacco or the expression *a pig in a poke* which dates back to the 1500s and refers to the idiocy of buying goods unseen. The pig hidden in a *poke* (concealed in a bag) might be of rather poor quality.

It would be interesting to know if the Norse word *poki* for a small pouch influenced the Irish word *póca* for a pocket. It seems possible given the widespread interactions between the two races and languages.

Race

A running *race* entered English around 1300 from the old Norse word *ras* (running or a rush of water). Old English has a similar word, *raes*, which may have merged with the Norse. Both came from the same Proto-Germanic root term *res* (to rage). Irish has a similar word, *rás* (*race*), possibly thanks to the same roots.

Race originally referred only to the act of running. The idea of a competitive speed contest only arose in the 1500s.

Rag

A scrap of cloth has been a *rag* since the 1300s (see *scrap*, below) and it probably comes from the Norse word *rögg* which described a shaggy tuft or from the Old Danish word *rag* with the same meaning. As an insulting word for a newspaper it dates to the 1700s and the concept of a *rags-to-riches* tale dates to 1896.

Raise

Raise (to set upright, build, or construct) has been a verb in English since 1200 from the Old Norse verb *reisa* (*to raise*). At first it shared its meaning with the original Old English verb *raeran* (to rear) but over time it evolved to have additional interpretations.

By the 1300s it had the idea of making something higher, including *raising* the volume of your voice, but also of restoring to life. From the 1500s you could describe the *raising of prices*. From the 1600s you could *raise a question* for discussion or *raise crops*. From the 1700s you could *raise children* and from the 1800s you could *raise your stake* in a game of cards. By the 1970s you might be more interested in *raising your consciousness.*

Raise is also a noun for an increase in pay since 1898, particularly in American English but that use is associated with other financial terms such as *raising a levy* or tax on a region or country (dating to the 1500s).

Rug & Rugged

Rug has been part of English since the 1550s, originally to name any coarse fabric, not necessarily those which lie on the floor. Old Norse had *rogg* (shaggy tuft) and Norwegian has *rugga* (coarse coverlet) so it's possible the original *rug* was thrown over a bed, rather than onto the floor.

By the 1590s the *rug* was a coverlet or wrap and by 1808 *rug* had made it to the floor from where it supplies a handful of evocative phrases to modern English.

Pull the rug out from under someone dates from 1936 in American English. Theatre slang took *rug* and turned it into a toupée in 1940. Slang gave us *cut a rug* for dancing in 1942 and *sweeping something under the rug* started in 1954.

The same roots give us the adjective *rugged* for somebody who looks shaggy or careworn.

Sale

Sale dates back to Old English when it was still spelled as *sala*. The act of selling something came from the Old Norse word *sala*. The idea of a *sale* being the act of selling something at a cheaper price than usual didn't arise until the 1800s which is probably just as well. The mental image of Vikings visiting Black Friday *sales* events is terrifying.

Scant

Scant, and derived words like *scantily* and *scantness*, entered English during the 1300s from Old Norse *skamt* (short or brief). It was also used as a noun in Middle English for scarcity or a *scant* supply.

Scrap

A leftover piece, a *scrap*, is an everyday word we've taken directly from the Vikings. In Old Norse you'll find *skrap* for *scraps* or trifles from the verb *skrapa* – to scrape, scratch or cut. The verb root suggests that the first *scraps* may have been leftovers from meat, hides, or fabrics.

Perhaps with this source the Vikings may even have given us the idea of *scrapbooking* in more recent times?

Scrape

The verb *scrape* comes from Old Norse *skrapa* (to *scrape*).

Scrub

Scrub, both as a verb and a noun, has Scandinavian roots. *Scrub* the verb entered English as *shrubben* around 1300, probably from the Danish *skrubbe* (*to scrub*). Used primarily about cleaning work, by 1828 it had acquired the sense of canceling something from the idea of erasing or rubbing out. The idea of *scrubbing* a mission stuck in air flight terminology from World War II and persists in space mission lingo.

The low growing bush or tree as a *scrub* was originally spelled as *shrobbe* in the 1300s again possibly from a Danish source – *shrub* (brushwood, a stunted tree). *Scrub* as slang for a servant or poor athlete arose in the 1500s but gained popularity from the late 1800s.

Seat

A *seat*, as in the object you sit on, came into English around 1200 from Old Norse *saeti* for the same idea. It's from a Proto-Germanic root word *saet* which also gives German its word for buttocks.

Ski

Ski is a relatively recent word in English (first use is recorded in 1883), indicating that it probably wasn't a direct gift from the Vikings. However historians believe primitive *skis* were invented 6,000 years ago by people living either in Scandinavia or Russia. By the Viking Age the Norse used them as an efficient way of travelling during their snowy winters.

They even worshipped Ullr, the god of *skiing*. Ullr was the stepson of Thor and specialised in hunting, skating, and *skiing* – all the fun winter pursuits of Norse culture.

Norwegian gifted the word *ski* to English. *Ski* was related to the Old Norse word *skid* (a long snowshoe) which translated literally as a stick of wood. You can read more about *skids* in the Fight Like a Viking chapter.

Skill

Skill has been a noun in English since the late 1100s when it first described the power of discernment. *Skill* came from the Old Norse word *skil* with the same meaning. Its Proto-Germanic roots also give us *skäl* in Swedish (reason), *skjel* in Danish (a boundary or limit), and *schele* in Dutch (discrimination) so the origins of *skill* appear to have been in the ability to judge and separate things.

The sense of *skill* denoting intelligence or ability didn't arise until the early 1200s and has been with us ever since.

Skip

The popular children's game of *skipping* has Norse roots. The word *skip* for leaping over comes from either Old Norse *skopa* (to take a run) or Middle Swedish *skuppa* (to *skip* or leap). The use of a *skipping rope* dates back to the 1600s and was a common game for both boys and girls until at least the 1900s. It's still a popular one in Irish school yards today.

Skirt

By the early 1300s the lower part of a woman's dress was being termed a *skirt* in English. *Skirt* came into the language from Old Norse *skyrta* which described a *shirt* or type of *kirtle*.

Kirtles aren't common today but they were a form of clothes popular with both women and men from the Middle Ages right up to the 1600s. A *kirtle* was worn over a smock (acting as a slip) and under the formal outer garment or coat.

The transition from *shirt* to *skirt* was probably aided by the long *shirts* worn by peasants in that period.

The expanded meaning of *outskirts* relating to the edges of town dates back to the late 1400s. By the 1550s *skirt* could be used to describe a collection of women in much the same way *suits* can be used to describe a collection of business men.

Sleuth

A *sleuth* in modern English is a detective, one who follows a trail of clues to catch the culprit. The idea of following a trail entwines through *sleuth's* word history.

Sleuth entered English around 1200 to describe the track or trail of a person. It came from the Old Norse word *slod* (trail). By the late 1300s the language had the idea of a *sleuth* being a type of bloodhound, a dog with a particularly good sense of smell and ability to track somebody.

By the 1840s a *sleuth* wasn't a dog anymore, but a person on the trail of another, a criminal other in this case. A *sleuth* became a keen investigator and a detective. The use of *sleuth* as a verb to describe the actions of a detective on the trail of a criminal arrived in the early 1900s, possibly as a result of the boom in early detective fiction in the late 1800s.

Snag

Hitting a *snag* is never a good thing in modern life. When buying a newly built house it is always wise to get a professional to check a *snag list* to identify any minor issues missed by the construction firm.

The verb *snag* in English generally relates to a boat catching on an unseen branch or stump underwater and this is closest to the early meaning of the word in English. In the 1570s *snag* entered English to describe a tree stump or branch probably from an Old Norse origin in *snagi* (a clothes peg) or *snag-hyrndr* (with sharp corners). A good Viking always watches out for *snags* under his longship, and a handy piece of wood to hang up his clothes.

Snug

Snug became an English word in the 1590s with a nautical usage. It meant that a ship was compact, trim, and well protected from the weather – something that Viking long ships struggled with as they had open decks with maybe a canvas shelter at best.

Despite that, the word *snug* is likely to come from Old Norse *snogger* (short haired), Old Swedish *snygg* (neat) or Old Danish *snøg* (tidy). This idea of *snugness* being a state of comfortable ease arose in the 1620s and that of fitting closely in 1838, although the compact ship would have the idea inherent in it too.

The original expression was *snug as a bee in a box* in 1706. Later we got *snug as a bug in a rug* in 1769.

Spike

Spike arrived in English around the mid 1300s as a large nail either from Old Norse *spik* (splinter) or Middle Swedish *spijk* (nail). It may also have been influenced from the Latin word *spica* (ear of grain) from the same root term *spei* (sharp point).

To *spike a gun* (1680s onwards) involved driving a large nail or *spike* into the touch hole of a cannon to prevent the gunpowder being ignited, *spiked* athletic shoes arrived in the 1830s, *spiking a story* before publication (1908) came from editors who stored rejected stories on a large desk *spike*, and adding alcohol to a drink to *spike* it arrived in the language in the late 1800s.

Stagger

The verb *stagger* came to English in the 1400s to describe walking unsteadily as a new version of the earlier word *stakeren*. *Stakeren* came from a Scandinavian source. It could have been *stagra* in Old Danish or *stakra* (to push, shove, or cause to reel) in Old Norse.

The idea of being *staggered* as a state of amazement and huge surprise didn't arise until the 1550s and arranging items in a a *staggered*, or zig-zag, pattern came along in the 1850s.

Suede

Suede, the soft underside of animal leathers is so named thanks to the French. When the fabric first became popular for making gloves in the 1800s they named it after its country of production – *gants de Suède* (gloves from Sweden).

When the soft finish became fashionable the name was shortened in English to just *suede*, thanks to its Swedish inventors.

Take

The verb *to take* has been described as one of the elemental words of the English language by no less a source than the Oxford English Dictionary, so it is intriguing to find its strong Viking roots.

Old English had a word for this idea before the Norse ships arrived – *niman* - and so did Middle English – *nimen*, both of which came from German and are related to the word *nimble*. However Old English acquired *tacan* (to take or seize) from Old Norse *taka* (see also *ta* in Swedish) and it gained supremacy quickly.

By around 1200 *take* didn't only mean to lay hold of something. It could be used for accepting something – *take advice*, for example, or to absorb – to *take a punch*. Additional meanings accumulated through the centuries. *Take the high road* (late 1200s), *take a shower, take sick, take the plunge, take it easy* (1880s), *take it or leave it* (1890s), *take five* (1929), *take the rap* (1930), and many more.

The connection of *take* with the idea of money earned or profits is surprisingly early, dating to the 1600s. A *take* in the world of movie-making arose in 1927 and the *take* from a performance is from shortly thereafter. The idea of somebody being open to bribery and *on the take* dates to the 1930s although bribery has been about much longer, of course.

Tangle

Tangle reached English from Scandinavian sources, probably either Swedish *taggla* (to disorder) or Old Norse *pongull* (seaweed) both of which come from seaweed root words, the idea being that seaweed *tangles* itself around oars and nets.

Western American English has the evocative slang *tanglefoot* to describe strong whiskey since 1859, presumably because it may cause a drinker's feet to become *tangled* and hence trip them.

Tatter

A *tatter* is a rag or scrap of fabric which also gives us the adjective *tattered* for worn clothing. It entered English around 1400 as *tatrys* (slashed garments) from Old Norse *töturr* (rags, *tattered* garments). It can also be used as a slang way to describe being tired – I'm in *tatters* - and is part of the 1600s word for a person, typically a street urchin, dressed in rags – a *tatterdemalion* - although that could come from tartar.

Them & They

Originally in Old English if you'd wanted to indicate a plural pronoun for somebody else (i.e. the third person plural pronoun) you would have said *him*. Around 1200 *him* was replaced by *them* for this use. It came from the Old Norse word *peim*.

Around the same time, and as part of the same language/grammar change, *they* replaced the Old

English *hi* and *hie* (plurals of he), *heo* (plural of she), and *hit* (plural of it). The Scandinavian forms were accepted with ease as they were more distinct than the Old English versions. Although they're small words, their widespread use may make them the most important Viking language imports of all.

From the late 1800s *they say* began to be used as a way of indicating that *it is said* by anonymous people of authority. Nobody knows who *they* are in this context. This is a huge shame as *they* have a lot to answer for.

Thrift

Thrift and *thrive* are more interconnected than you might imagine and both have Viking roots. *Thrift* has been a noun in English since 1300 when it meant the condition of thriving or to have savings. It came from the Middle English verb *thriven* (*to thrive*, as you might guess). *Thriven* either came from, or was heavily influenced by, the Old Norse word *þrift* which related to *thriving* and prosperity.

From the 1500s the idea of *thrift* became more linked with the notion of saving money, often by seeking out good value and living in an economical way. So by the 1520s you might describe somebody as being *thrifty* in this way. The flip side, of course, was a *spendthrift* who spent recklessly. Other terms for a *spendthrift* included a *scattergood* or a *spend-all*.

By the early 1900s the idea of a *thrift shop* had arrived and now you can use *thrifting* as a verb to describe going shopping in *thrift* shops (goodwill stores in American English) in search of good value bargains.

Thrive

To *thrive* is to be healthy and successful in life and it is a concept taken into English from a Scandinavian source around 1200, probably from Old Norse *prifask* (to *thrive*).

Prifask came from the idea of grasping to yourself because *prifa* was the verb for clutching, grasping, and taking hold. There are related words in Norwegian (*triva* – to seize), Swedish (*trifvas*), and Danish *trives* (to *thrive* or flourish). It may say something about Viking culture that the idea of getting and holding something was the ideal of success in life.

Tidings

Tidings is a somewhat old-fashioned word for news which has faint echoes of a time when the sea was more obvious in life than it is now.

Time and *tide* were closely linked in the past. When clocks and watches were less prevalent in the world the person most concerned with the time was the ship's captain who watched with care for the next *tide* to carry his ship into or from harbour. As a result the idea of *tide* and time were closely linked and sometimes used interchangeably.

Equally most news arrived by ship. Many people lived and died within a few miles of the village of their birth but sailors carried news from foreign shores and faraway places so news often arrived on the *tide* too.

Tidings (an announcement of an event) entered English around 1200 as *tidung* (event or news) – partly from the Old English verb *tidan* (to happen) and partly from Old

Norse *tidendi* (events, news) from a Proto-Germanic root word relating to division of time. The same roots provide words for news and newspaper in Norwegian, German, and Dutch.

Time

Time entered English as Old English *tima* (a limited space of *time*) which has roots in Old Norse *timi* (proper time) and Swedish *timme* (an hour).

The concept of *time* as an infinite abstract idea dates to the 1300s and by 1509 there were images of an old man carrying an hour glass and scythe to personify *time*.

Time works harder as a word in English than in other European languages. *Time* in English can mean the extent of *time*, a specific point in *time*, and an hour. Whereas in French you'd have *temps, fois* and *heure* for those ideas and in German you've *Zeit, Mal*, and *Uhr*.

"The Times" as the name of a newspaper dates to 1788. *Time* in science fiction has always been important. The first *time-traveling* story was "The Time Machine" by H.G. Wells and the first *time* capsule was created in 1938 for the New York World Fair.

Although *time* reached England with the Norse invaders, the wearing of *time* pieces wasn't important in a largely agricultural society until the arrival of the train, the *timetable*, and the industrial revolution. The idea of *being on time* arose in 1854 as a result of the railroads.

To *do time* (serve a prison sentence) first appeared in 1865. The phrase *in the nick of time* dates to Tudor times and the *nick* in question is the precise mark or notch on a wooden tally stick, an early method of recording quantities precisely. The earlier phrase for the same concept was *pudding time*. Pudding (dessert) was served first so if you arrived in *time* for that course, you were *just in time.*

Until

This preposition (in English since around 1200) is actually formed by joining together two earlier prepositions, both with roughly the same meaning. Similar words occur in Swedish (*intill*) and Danish (*indtil*).

Un is the first part and it means up to and as far as. You will also find it in *unto* with the same objective. *Un* came from Old Norse *und*.

Til (to), is the second part and it came to Old English (especially in Northumbrian) from the Old Norse word *til* (to, *until*). It was a common preposition in various Scandinavian languages. The word is lost there now but leaves traces of connections to endings, goals, and death.

Wag

A dog's *wagging* tail has a strange backstory. *Wag* entered English in the early 1200s as a verb to describe vacillation and lack of steadfastness. It came from a Scandinavian source for a different idea – rocking a cradle. Old Norse had *vagga* (a cradle), Danish has *vugge* (rock a cradle), and Old Swedish had *wagga* for the same notion. All of them have the same Proto-Germanic root but it was about moving in a vehicle rather than a baby in a rocking cradle.

From the mid 1400s *wag* had left behind the idea of rocking a cradle and become associated with the happy motion of a dog's tail.

Wag has spawned a wide variety of words and phrases since then. There was a *waghalter* – somebody who is destined to swing from the gallows. This was possibly shortened to give us *wag* (1550s) for somebody who loves making jokes. There was also a *wagger* (late 1300s) – somebody who stirs up trouble. From the late 1800s you might also encounter a *wag-at-the-wall* – a wall clock whose weights and pendulum are exposed to view.

Want

Want as both a noun (a shortage of something) and as a verb (to desire something) entered English at the same time, 1200, both from Viking roots.

The verb comes from Old Norse *vanta* (to lack or *want*). Initially it related to not having something but by the 1700s it was most often being used to describe the act of wishing for or desiring something.

The noun comes from Old Norse *vant*. The idea of a shortage soon came to be associated with a state of poverty. The idea of a *want ad* arose in the late 1800s.

Weak

Weak entered English from the Old Norse word *veikr* (*weak*) around 1300.

Window

Window has been an English word since 1200 as a direct adoption from the Old Norse *vindauga* which is compounded from *vindir* (air or wind) and *auga* (eye).

Window replaced the Old English words *eagthyrel* (eye hole) and *eagduru* (eye door). The idea of a *window* being like a door was common in languages of northern Europe at that time – both were openings in the structure of a building. In Old Frisian, for example, you had *andern* for window which translates as breath-door.

A *window* was originally an unglazed hole in the roof which adds a little more sense to terms like wind-eye or breath-door as presumably they were mostly there to allow smoke from fires to escape.

The Swedes have abandoned the Norse word for window in favour of *fönster* from the German *fenster* (with Latin roots) and even English retained *fenester* as a parallel word until the 1500s but Danish still has a very similar *window* word today (*vindue*).

The Latin rooted *fenester* in English only persists in the fun 1600s word *defenestration*, the act of throwing somebody out of a window.

Perhaps thanks to the wider availability of glazing, *window* phrases mostly date from the 1800s onwards in English. *Window* seat is one of the earliest (1778) but after that we get *window dressing* (1853), *window shopping* (1904), and *window of opportunity* (1979) which arose from the precious and often fleeting *launch windows* of the American space flight programme.

Wing

Wing entered English in the late 1100s as *wenge* from the Old Norse word *vaengr* (the *wing* of a bird).

As early as 1400s, *wing* was being used to describe two parts of the same political party or army and by the 1790s it had acquired its theatrical meaning about the sides of a stage.

To be under someone's wing in a protective or mentoring sense arrived in early 1200s.

The phrase *on a wing and prayer* is the title of 1943 song about landing a damaged aircraft. The idea of *winging it* may come from observations of baby birds trying to take flight but theatrical legend has it that it was from an actor learning their lines at the last minute in the *wings* of the stage or being fed their lines from a prompter in the *wings*. The truth may never be known.

Wrong

This Late Old English word for something which is twisted or crooked comes from Old Norse *rangr* (crooked, *wrong).* The idea of crookedness being *wrong* is also present in Latin where *right* comes from *rectus* (right or straight) and *pravus* was *wrong* but literally translated as crooked. The same concept applies in Italian and Slavic.

Wrong came to have a more moral meaning of unjust from the 1300s and that's when the idea of a *wrong-doer* joined the dictionary too. To be on *the wrong side* of a certain age (i.e. older than) arose in the 1660s and *to get up on the wrong side of the bed* became a problem in 1801.

13. The Norse Landscape

Unlike the Anglo-Saxons of the time, Vikings travelled both widely and often. They encountered a wide variety of lands and peoples. Hence they needed words to describe what they saw whether to teach navigation, give directions, or bring home tales of what they had found on their voyages. As a result they gave a number of landscape, geographic, and weather words to the English language as it evolved from the 700s to 1050.

While some words here are relatively rare in English now (*haggard, holm, ness,* and *beck*), others deserve a comeback (*glocken*), and several are so everyday that most English speakers will have no idea they owe a debt to the Vikings (*fog, low,* and *sky*).

Bank (of a river)

Bank as the name for the land bordering a river arrived in English around 1200 from either Old Norse *banki* or Old Danish *banke* (sandbank). There may have been an Old English word for the same thing, but it hasn't survived.

Bank in the financial sense has Italian roots.

Beck

A *beck* is a stream and while not used widely in English today outside of poetry books, you will find it in place names - Tooting Bec in London and Beckholme, for example.

Beck entered English in the 1300s as *bek* in Middle English from the Old Norse word *bekkr*. It is unrelated to *beckon*.

Fell

A *fell* is a rocky hill and mostly remains in English thanks to place names. For example, Scafell Pike is the highest mountain in England. *Fell running*, which originated in the Lake District in England, is the sport of running in the mountains.

Fell entered English around 1300 from the Old Norse word *fiall* (mountain). This type of *fell* is unrelated to the past tense of the verb *to fall* or to the phrase *one fell swoop* (first used in the play "Macbeth").

Fjord

Fjord entered English in the 1600s from the Norwegian word *fjord* and its own roots are in Proto-Germanic *ferthuz* – a place for crossing over, a ford.

A *firth*, describing an estuary of the sea in Scotland came unsurprisingly from Scottish to English in the early 1400s, probably from the Old Norse word *fjordr* for *fjord*.

Flat

The adjective *flat* to describe something which is level, even, and smooth arrived in English in the mid 1300s from the Old Norse word *flatr* (*flat*). Its meaning expanded in the centuries thereafter.

By the 1500s something *flat* might be dull and featureless and musical notes could be *flat* if lower than the intended pitch.

By the 1600s a drink could be *flat*.

By the 1800s a woman's bosom might be *flat* and in 1876 the idea of *flat-earth* was used to describe those refusing to accept the idea of a globe-shaped planet Earth.

Flat in the 1900s could be a good thing or a bad thing. A *flat tyre* (or tire) was an issue from 1908 but a *flat-screen* (1969) wasn't so bad.

Note – a *flat*, as in an apartment, comes from a different linguistic source.

Fog

Fog entered English in the 1500s to describe thick, obscuring mist from a Scandinavian source – either *fog* in Danish (spray, shower, or snowdrift) or Norse *fjuk* (a drifting snowstorm). The idea of being *in a fog* as a way of describing being lost and unable to decide what to do next arose in English in the 1600s.

Glocken

According to "The Little Book of Snow" by Sally Coulthard *glocken* is an Old Yorkshire dialect word for the point at which snow starts to thaw. I can't think of a mainstream English word for this state of affairs, so we may need to adopt this one. *Glocken*, like many words in Old Yorkshire dialect comes from Viking roots. It comes from the Icelandic *glöggur* (to make clear). Another charmingly chilly word in this dialect is *ice-shoggles* (icicles).

Haggard

Haggard is best known now as an adjective for looking careworn or gaunt and in that guise it's from French words relating to falconry or possibly from German words about hedges. To be told you look "like you've been dragged through a hedge backwards" is another way to comment on your *haggard* looks so perhaps the hedge link is correct.

However a *haggard* is also a word, primarily surviving in Ireland and on the Isle of Man, for a particular area on a farm and it survives in traditional field names. The *haggard* was an enclosed area close to the farmyard used for stacking grain or fodder for animals. It's believed that the word comes from the Old Norse *heygarthr*, a compound word formed from *hey* (hay) and *garthr* (yard).

Holm

Holm is a mostly obsolete English word now whose meaning was a small island in a river or a river meadow. This Late Old English word came from Old Norse *holmr* (small island, especially in a river or bay). *Holm* is preserved in various place names such as *Holmbush* and Durham (originally *Dun Holm*).

Knoll

Knoll, a low hill, was originally spelled as *cnoll* in Old English and arrived via Old Norse *knollr* (hilltop). Related words include German's *knolle* for a clod or lump. While Dutch either has *knol* (turnip) or *nol* (a hill).

Probably the most famous *knoll* in history is the *grassy knoll* so beloved of conspiracy theorists around the assassination of U.S. President John F. Kennedy in 1963, which has become a tourist destination in Dallas, Texas.

Low

Low, as something below the usual level or near the ground, wasn't a word in Old English so it's assumed it entered English from Old Norse *lagr* (*low*, short, humble).

Low was a useful word when it did arrive and rapidly came to have meanings unrelated to the landscape. *Low* referred to areas near the coast as early as 1300 and gave us the *Low Countries* for Belgium, the Netherlands, and Luxembourg from the 1540s. *Low* in a musical pitch sense arose in 1300, humble in rank from 1200, and *low* in character from the 1500s.

Lying low to avoid being seen was being done as early as the mid 1200s. *Low prices* were sought around the same time and *feeling low* arose in the 1700s. A *low blow*, as you might guess, came to the dictionary from boxing in the 1940s.

Muggy

Now used in describing weather which is close and humid with plenty of moisture in the air, the word *muggy* entered English in the 1700s by joining the now obsolete word Middle English word *mug* with the *-y* suffix. A *mug* wasn't just a drinking vessel back then but was a term for a fog or mist.

Middle English had the verb *mugen* (to drizzle with fog or mist) from the late 1300s from the Old Norse word *muggy* (drizzling mist).

Muggy weather and a drinking *mug* both have Viking roots, but come from different Old Norse words. You can read about *mug's* history in the Fight Like a Viking chapter.

Ness

A *ness* is a point of land which runs out into the sea but it is largely lost to English now except in place names (think of Caithness in Scotland and Skegness in England, for example) and as a surname. It was originally spelled as *naes* in Old English and may have arrived via a link to *nasu*, the Old English word for a nose. *Ness* arrived from Old Norse *nes* and Danish *naes*.

This promontory *ness* is unrelated to -*ness* the suffix in words like *goodness*, *kindness* etc.. Loch *Ness* in Scotland, and possible home to legendary creature *Nessie*, is probably unrelated also. Loch *Ness* was originally named *Nis* in Scots Gaelic and that means *now* in that language. However some experts suspect its name may come from the now extinct Pictish language which pre-dates the Vikings.

Rim

The link between *rim* and landscape is obscure, but does make sense when explained.

Rim was originally *rima* in Old English and it meant an edge, border, or coast. This idea of boundary was explicit in the related Old English words *saerima*, or seashore, literally the *rim* of the sea, and *daegrima* – dawn or the *rim* of the day. Anybody viewing a sunrise over the horizon of the sea can see how it resembles an edge or *rim*.

Rima is likely to have come from the Old Norse word *rime*, a raised strip of land or a ridge. It's also in Old Frisian as *rim* for edge but doesn't appear in other languages.

Sky

The English word for *sky* is a direct import of the Old Norse word for cloud. What this tells us about the weather in Viking countries versus the British Isles is debatable.

The original Saxon/British word would have been *heofen*, which is related to the idea of *Heaven*. In Middle English *sky* was used interchangeably for the concept of a religious *heaven* and for the upper regions of the air above us. By the 1800s and 1900s *sky* had given us other airy ideas such as *sky-high* (1812), *the sky's the limit* (1908), *sky dive* (1965), and even *sky writing* (1922).

14. Viking Beliefs

Thanks to the rich resource of the Viking sagas and other accounts written after the Vikings converted to Christianity, historians have a pretty good idea of what the average Viking believed, although not all the details. The basics included a group of male and female *Asgardian* gods presided over by Odin, frost giants, the nine worlds, Yggdrasil the World Tree, and more.

This chapter also covers their everyday beliefs and customs, and answers some curious questions about the minor Norse beliefs and superstitions. Did Vikings think *dreams* had meanings? Yes. Did they play pranks on *April Fool's Day*? Probably. Did they place a coin in a new purse to invite good fortune? Yes.

The Vikings also, like the Egyptians and the Japanese, believed their early monarchs were at least part divine. According to legend the first King of Sweden was Fjolnir. He was the son of the Vanir god Frey and his wife Gerd the giant. Poor Fjolnir came to tragic end. He drowned in a large vat of mead late at night while hunting in the darkness for somewhere to relieve himself. A truly vital lesson there on the importance of indoor plumbing.

Key Viking beliefs like *Asgard, Ragnarok* (the grim Viking view of the end of time), *Valkryies*, and *Valhalla* are all here. Perhaps more surprising given their differing religions are the words the Vikings gave to the Christian Anglo Saxons they settled amongst. *Awe, cross, hell*, and *heathen* are all here although often the Vikings gave these words different meanings to the ones which persisted into modern English. The Saxons even have the Vikings to thank for the Christmas tradition of drinking a *wassail*.

Asgard

Thanks to the Thor movies by Marvel, nearly everybody knows *Asgard* is where the Viking gods dwelled so this word is obviously one the Vikings gave us. The word is a compounding of *ass* (god) in Old Norse with *gardr* (enclosure or garden).

Asgard wasn't just for gods and goddesses however, heroes slain in battle also gained the right to live there. According to Norse religion *Asgard* is one of the nine worlds, ruled by Odin and his wife Frigg. *Valhalla*, where the slain heroes feast and fight forever, is located in *Asgard*.

Asgard was generally regarded as being in the sky and was connected to the world of humans (*Midgard*) via the *Bifrost*, a rainbow bridge.

Awe & Awesome

Awe, originally spelled as *aghe* and later as *aue*, joined English in 1200 to describe feelings of fear and terror. The word came from Old Norse *agi* (fright) with related words for fear in many Germanic languages.

The association of *awe* with religious respect didn't arise until much later, thanks to Biblical references. The *phrase to stand in awe* was originally simply *to stand awe*.

Ultimately this means that when, since 1960, we say something is *awesome*, we're quoting the Vikings and technically it means the thing is scary rather than inspiring and impressive.

Cross

Although Christianity primarily came to the Vikings from the British Isles, the Vikings gave the English language the word for *cross*, with a little help from the Romans and the Irish.

The *cross*, as a symbol of the crucifixion, was massively important to the residents of the Britain and Ireland before the arrival of the first Viking raiders but the original Old English word for the *cross* was *rood*, a word for a pole, particularly in this case one used in punishments.

Then around 950, Old English got the word *cros* from Old Norse. The Vikings had acquired the word from either Old Irish *cros* or from Latin *crux* (stake for hanging criminals) which is the source for the word in Italian, French, Spanish, Dutch, and German.

By 1200 *cross* was being used to describe a *cross-shaped* object, the making of the *sign of the cross* by Christians, or any burden or penance suffered in the name of the Christian religion.

Dream

Given that the Vikings gave us the word *nightmare* (see below) it's appropriate that they had a hand in the idea of a *dream* too.

The images which pass through a sleeping person's mind at rest became an English word during the 1200s from the Old Norse word *draumr*. There are related words in many Scandinavian languages – Danish (*drøm*), Swedish (*dröm*) plus Old Frisian, High German, and Dutch.

Dream (or *dreman*) was a word in Old English before the arrival of the Vikings but it had a totally different meaning – joy, merriment, noise, and music. That original meaning faded to oblivion during the Middle English phase of the language's development.

Vikings treated *dreams* with serious respect. While some they dismissed as *draum-skrok* (nonsense) others were believed to foretell the future. Some leaders had, or claimed to have, prophetic *dreams* of establishing kingdoms and conquering lands. Even the Viking gods believed in the strength of *dreams* to predict their fates.

In other stories the *dreams* were a way for humans to contact gods, elves, spirits, and the dead. Seers were often consulted to help interpret significant *dreams* and if such dreams were sought the sleeper might choose to rest on a grave mound or a special animal hide in order to induce a *dream* to guide them in future actions in the waking world.

Flit

Flit entered English around 1200 as *flitten, flytten*, and *flutten*. It took a while to settle on a spelling form. *Flit* meant to move something from one place to another and it came from the Old Norse word *flytja* (to move or migrate).

By the 1500s *flit* had come to mean the removal from one place of habitation to another, particularly in northern English and Scottish so it's perhaps unsurprising that my first experience of this word came from my mother who has Scottish ancestry. Her superstition was that it was ill-luck to move house or lodging on a Saturday as "*Saturday flitting is short sitting*".

Consensus on this belief is hard to find as a 1641 farming book by Henry Best advises "*Munday flitte, Neaver sitte*". Perhaps a Tuesday might be best?

Flit also gives us the noun *flitting* (a household removal) since 1835.

My mother-in-law adheres to a variation on this belief about Saturday *flitting*, which is medical rather than residential. She believes that it's unlucky to be discharged from hospital on a Saturday as you will soon need to return for further treatment.

Fool & April Fool's Day

Fool became an English word in the early 1200s to denote a silly or stupid person. It came from the Old French word *fol* (idiot, jester, or rogue). How it arrived in French is open to debate.

Medieval Latin had the word *follus* (foolish) drawn from Latin *follis* (bellows) which drew on the idea of a windbag being full of air, perhaps with the puffed out cheeks of a buffoon.

It is likely that the Latin word was borrowed by the Vikings as Old Norse had *fol* and Old Danish had *fool* and that may have been how it transferred into Old French and finally into English.

Shortly after its arrival in English a *fool* was used to describe a court jester and by the early 1300s some churches celebrated the *Feast of Fools* on New Year's Day. The expression *no fool like an old fool* arose in 1546 and *to make a fool of somebody* was possible by the 1600s.

We may even have the Vikings to thank for the term *April Fool's Day* as the original term for it was *April-gawk* (from the 1600s) where a *gawk* was drawn from *gaukr*, the Old Norse word for a cuckoo.

The tradition of sending people on foolish errands and playing pranks came to England from France in the late 1600s. In northern England (a heartland for Viking customs and language influence) *April Fool's Day* was traditionally the 1st of May rather than the first of April and might have been associated with the cuckoo bird whose first calls of spring are often heard during late April or early May. Interestingly the *fool* in this northern tradition was called the *May gosling*.

The French version of *April Fool's Day* is called *Poisson d'Avril* (April's fish) and involves trying to attach paper (or real!) fish to as many unwitting victims as possible. How French fish turned into English cuckoos is unknown.

Handsel

Handsel (or *hansel*) isn't a particularly common English word but it's used in my family and has Norse roots. When I was younger, every time my mother (who is of Scottish descent, way back) gave me a purse, bag, or wallet (or I bought one for myself) she insisted on placing a coin inside it for good fortune and she called this *hanselling*. The tradition is often passed from mother to daughter and is still observed by some in Ireland, Britain, Australia, Newfoundland, and elsewhere, sometimes without knowing the word or its origins.

The idea of *handselling* a purse is a British tradition dating back to at least 1050A.D. The word itself was used in Saxon and in Danish and means "to deliver into the hand". It's unclear if the Saxons gave this to the Vikings, or vice versa.

There's even a *Handsel Day* when tips and gifts are expected by servants, postmen etc. Money is the traditional gift but others are permitted so long as they aren't sharp as that would cut the relationship. Over time *Handsel Day* was supplanted by the similar traditions on Boxing Day (26th of December) in Britain. Thanks to disputes over the Julian and the Gregorian calendars you may celebrate *Handsel Day* on the first Monday in January or *Auld Handsel Day* on the first Monday after the 12th of January.

Some references to this tradition link it to summoning spells, so be wary of the person giving you that coin in your new purse.

Heathen

Given the way Vikings and the native English interacted over religion it is appropriate that both languages merged to produce the word *heathen* and particularly appropriate that both races used it with a different meaning.

182

Old English had the word *haeden* (not Christian, Jewish, or Muslim). They used it to describe any person, race, or nation who did not acknowledge the god of the New Testament. They particularly used it to describe the Danish Vikings who first raided their shores and then settled there. It probably didn't help that the Vikings saw Christian religious communities, and their gold, as easy pickings.

More surprising is that Old Norse had a similar word – *heidinn* (heathen or pagan). This merged with the Old English word to give us *heathen*.

So who would a Viking have called *heathen*? Somebody who didn't acknowledge the power of Odin and the Asgardians?

In fact the Viking word is influenced by the bible again. It is likely to be a word chosen by Ulfilas when he first translated the bible into a Germanic language and needed a word to describe a gentile woman. It may even be a literal translation of somebody who lives on a *heath* (open common moorland and hence part of the main community). It was either a Greek borrowing/adaption or chosen because it sounds like the Greek word for the same concept. Ulfilas was a missionary around 350 who led a team of translators to create a Bible which could be used in the Gothic conversions to christianity. He was the son of parents enslaved by the Goths.

Viking use of the word *heathen* wouldn't have been the same was its use by Anglo Saxons. The Christians would use it in a negative sense to mark out those who didn't follow the correct religion (i.e. theirs), whereas for the Vikings it would have been a neutral word to refer to each other as being part of the same community.

Hell

Hell has been in the English language since Old English as *hel* or *helle* so its spelling has varied over time as most older words do. Old Norse had *hel* too, so the link is clear. The idea of a world for the dead and a place of torment for the wicked was common across many countries at the time. Often perceived as an underworld it may be connected to Old Norse *hellir* – a cave or cavern.

The Norse mythological *Hel* was the name of Loki's daughter. She ruled over Niflheim, the lowest of all the nine worlds and the place where the evil dead go. Nifl meant mist, which provides an image of the spot, which was sometimes said to be guarded by a giant hound called Garm, like Cerberus guarding the underworld in Greek mythology.

There were several different afterworlds in the Norse belief system. Valhalla for warriors, Folkvang, the underwater hall of the giantess Ran for those lost at sea, and *Hel* for those who died of natural causes rather than in battle. None of them were connected directly to your pious behaviour in the living world, unlike the Christian concept of *hell*.

The dead in *Hel* continued to eat, drink, fight, and sleep. It wasn't bliss or torment. It was continued life, but elsewhere. Old Norse sources describe *Helvegr* in detail, this was the road to *Hel* and may have come from shamanic style journeys similar to other peoples living around the Arctic Circle. The road was taken by gods and humans to recover a dead spirit or talk to the dead. Part of the trip involved crossing the River Gjoll (made of clanging weapons rather than water), again like Greek mythology.

Hell has contributed many expressions to the English language. By the 1300s it could be used to describe any bad experience. *Hell break loose* arrived in the 1630s. *Hell in a hand-basket* (meaning an easy journey) arose in the 1800s as did *hell and high water*. Shakespeare gave us *go to hell* in the "Merchant of Venice".

We've also got *til hell freezes over* (1832), *snowball's chance in hell* (1931), *for the hell of it* (1921), and *hell for leather* – referring to sliding around on a leather horse saddle (1889).

Kirk

Kirk is an old word in English for a church, mostly used in northern England and Scotland now. English acquired it around 1200 from Old Norse *kirkja* (church).

Kirk is a widespread element in place names for this reason – *Falkirk, Selkirk*, and many others in Scotland, and *Dunkirk* in France, for example.

Nightmare

Nightmare's word origins are widespread across Germanic, Scandinavian, and Slavic countries but it reached English around 1300 (originally spelled as *niht-genga*) to describe an evil female spirit who gave sleepers a feeling of suffocation in their chest. This idea of a night dwelling goblin on your chest persisted for centuries until it came to describe all bad dreams during the 1800s. Around the same time it could be used to describe any bad experience, even one you have when you're awake.

Middle Dutch has a similar word *nachtmare*, German has *Nachtmahr*, and French drew its own word *cauchemar* from those sources. In Swedish the demon in question is called a *mara* and it was the same in Old Icelandic.

The Vikings contributed to *nightmare* history via the sagas. In the *Ynglingasaga*, written in Old Norse by the Icelandic poet Snorri Sturluson around 1225 (translated into English in 1844), the *mara* causes the death of King Vanlandi. The attack has been caused via witchcraft with the king being overcome by sleep yet sensing a presence in his chamber. The *mara's* weight is so heavy that first it crushes his legs and then kills him. Modern doctors consider it likely that this form of *nightmares*, which were widely reported across Europe and beyond for centuries, may have been cases of sleep paralysis where the victim is awake and aware of their surroundings but totally unable to move.

According to folklore one way to confuse a *mara* was to place your shoes or slippers by your bed in the wrong order - the right where the left should be and vice versa. Another way was to hang mistletoe under the roof.

Ragnarok

Ragnarok is the end of the world in the Norse belief system. It is predicted to be the last battle of the world when men and gods alike will be destroyed by monsters and darkness. The word comes from Old Norse and is a combination of two terms – *ragna* (gods) and either *rök* (end) or *rökr* (twilight).

How *Ragnarok* was expected to unfold goes something like the following. One day, as the fates decide, the sun will fail and the Great Winter will result. The struggle for survival will cause brother to turn on brother. The stars will disappear and mountains will fall. Monsters of Viking legends will break free of their bonds.

Meanwhile in Asgard, fire giants will invade. Odin and his gods will fight them, despite knowing it will be in vain. All will fail and the world will sink back into the sea. Creation will be undone.

Clearly not a cheerful bedtime story, although variations exist where this annihilation is followed by a rebirth of the world. It's possible these were later versions influenced by Christian teachings of rebirth reaching into the Viking world.

Summer

Summer is the growing season in the northern hemisphere and an important season to both the Vikings and the Saxons. *Summer* comes from the Old English term *sumnor* and it has very old roots. There's a root word *sem* which produces *sama* in Sanskrit and *sam* in Old Irish. There's another root word in Proto-Germanic, *sumra*, which led to *sumar* in Old Norse and Old Saxon (and *zomer* in Dutch and *Sommer* in German). It's interesting that the same word was in Norse and Saxon. It's impossible to say definitely that the Vikings brought *summer* to the Saxons and hence to English, but it's certainly possible.

The Norse also observed *sumarsdag*, the first day of *summer*, on the Thursday that fell between April 9th and 15th so *summer* was important to them with the long daylight hours important in contrast with the long, dark winters.

Celebrations of *midsummer* (and *midsummer eve*) are still important in Scandinavian countries today, with special parties, family gatherings, weddings, maypoles, flower wreaths, and bonfires.

Valhalla

Valhalla appears to have entered English in the 1600s when historians discussed Norse sagas in their textbooks but given the importance of *Valhalla* to Vikings and the centuries they spent settled and inter-marrying in Ireland and England, it is highly likely that the word was understood in the British Isles long before then and the 1600s use was a re-introduction.

Valhalla comes from the Old Norse *Valhöll* (hall of the battle-slain). *Valhalla* was the hall in Asgard where Odin receives the souls of heroes who have fallen in battle. Dying of old age after many victorious battles wouldn't be enough.

According to Norse poetry its roof is made of shields resting on rafters made of spears, the seats are breastplates and wolves guard its gates. Life in *Valhalla* is the ideal for Viking warriors. All day they fight each and gain honour but at sunset their wounds are healed and they feast all night, served by Valkyries (see below) with excellent food and mead. This blissful life won't be eternal however. Odin gathers them to support him during the battle at the end of the world, Ragnarok (see above).

Valkyrie

Like Valhalla, this Viking word was probably in English long before it was re-introduced by historians in the 1700s. In fact Anglo Saxon tales had their own version of the war-maidens, the *waelcyrie*, but they had a much larger role in Scandinavian legends and mythology. Similarly the Celts had war goddesses Badb, Ériu (who gave her name to Éire and Ireland), and the Morrigan fulfilling a similar role in their legends.

There were twelve *valkyries*. They escorted those slain in battle, and deemed worthy by Odin, to Valhalla in Asgard. In Old Norse they were called *valkyria* (choosers of the slain). Once in Valhalla the maidens served the heroes in their feasting.

Earlier Norse tales lend the *valkyries* a darker side. Their responsibilities, as helpers to Odin, involved choosing who would die in battle. When needed they used dark magic to achieve these deaths. One saga show them weaving the fates of the warriors before the battle. Their loom wasn't standard, however. Their thread was human intestines, the weights were severed heads, and swords and arrows were their weaving tools.

The German composer Wilhelm Richard Wagner perhaps ensured the continuation of the myths of the valkyries when he scored the famous "Ride of the *Valkyries*" section of his masterpiece the Nibelungen Ring of four operas which were loosely based on the Viking sagas. Most famously used in "Apocalypse Now" the music has appeared in many movies and television programmes including "The Big Bang Theory", "The Simpsons" and, "The Blue Brothers".

Wand

Vikings did believe in magic, but not the variety that requires a *wand*. Despite that they are responsible for the word *wand* in the English dictionary.

Wand joined English around 1200 from the Old Norse word *vondr* (rod or switch/animal whip). It wasn't anything to do with magic originally, it was just a flexible stick. It was probably used to describe the type of sticks and branches used in weaving walls and animal enclosure fences. Two centuries later, in the 1400s, the words *magic* and *wand* are used together and hey presto!

Wassail

Admittedly *wassail* isn't a commonly used English word but this one was too good to omit.

Wassail joined English in the mid 1100s as a compound of two Old Norse words – *ves* (be) and *heill* (healthy). Essentially it was a toast to your health, similar to many others in languages around the globe. It appears to have been common amongst the Danes living in England at this period and spread from there to the native inhabitants.

The meaning of *wassail* expanded around 1300 to include the alcohol in which healths are drunk, particularly the spiced ale used for such toasts at Christmas Eve celebrations. By 1600 *wassailing* described revelling and from 1742 it was a Christmas tradition to go from house to house singing carols and being rewarded with a sip from the communal *wassail* cup which was filled with hot mulled cider. This tradition was performed on Christmas Eve, New Year's Eve, and on 12th night.

The early Vikings may not have been Christian but their toast influenced the way Christians celebrated the season.

The second version of *wassailing* is performed in the apple-growing regions of England. The idea is that at the end of the year you make up your cider-based *wassail* tipple and bring it, along with a rowdy group of orchard workers, out to the apple orchard where you sing and make as much noise as possible around the trees, presumably to wake them for a new season of growth. One tree in particular is named the king of the orchard. Then some of the *wassail* is poured around its roots as an offering for a good harvest in the next season.

15. Salmagundi

Salmagundi is one of my favourite words. It describes a type of dish, rather than a specific recipe. The idea is that a *salmagundi* is a platter of food of many different types all arranged together, possibly with a dressing. The most basic version was boiled salt fish with onions but it could also contain chopped meat, eggs, and anything which was available to the chef. *Salmagundi* is the perfect dish for when stores are low, on a longship nearing the end of its voyage, for example.

Here's the *salmagundi* of Viking words and phrases which defied my efforts to stow them in previous chapters. They are unique, individual, and far too good to omit from this volume. From *akimbo* to *freckle, slang, glitter,* and *trash* you'd never guess they are Viking terms, but they deserve celebration.

Akimbo

Akimbo, standing with your hands on your hips and elbows bent outwards, entered Middle English as in *kenebowe* and its origins are disputed but worth exploration.

One possibility is the word came from *keen* (sharp) and *bow* (arch) in Middle English itself. Others point towards the teapot analogy present in many languages for this posture. For example, in French you'd say somebody was *faire le pot a deux anses* (to play the pot with two handles) and in Old French you had *kane* for pot which might lead to *kenebowe*, and later *akimbo*.

The third possibility is Scandinavian, a lost word something like *kengboginn* in Icelandic which means bow-bent. It's worth noting that a) elbows at that angle do resemble archery bows in use and b) *akimbo* originally had a second meaning of somebody sitting in a bowed over position.

The language jury is out, but there's a good chance the Vikings gave us *akimbo*.

Dandruff

Dandruff is the dry scales or dust which forms on the scalp and then falls onto the shoulders. The full etymology of the word is obscure but part of it has Viking roots, which provides an amusing mental image of Viking warriors and shield maidens fussing over their hair between battles and raids.

The *dand* part of the compound hasn't been traced to a source yet but the *ruff* part comes from Northumbrian or East Anglian dialect words *huff* and *hurf* (scab). Those areas of Britain were heavily settled by Danish Vikings. *Hurf* and *huff* come from Old *Norse hrufa* which has Proto-Germanic roots in a term which gives other languages their words for leper.

Droopy

Being *droopy* is to be in a sad, dejected, gloomy state of mind and it dates to the 1200s when it was spelled *drupie*. It is likely to have come from the Old Norse word *drupr* which described faintness and drooping spirits, or from the related Old Norse word *drupa* – to drop or hang your head.

Even Vikings got the blues.

Freckle

Freckle, and its early spelling variants *frecken* and *frackens* entered Old English in the 1300s. You'll find them in Chaucer's "Knight's Tale" in "The Canterbury Tales". They came from *freknur* the Old Norse plural noun for those sun-induced skin dapplings.

Freknur was also the source for *frekna* (Icelandic), *fregne* (Danish), and *frägne* (Swedish).

It would be fun to imagine that *freckles* arrived on the pale-skinned Vikings themselves as they inter-married with nationalities living further south from their home fjords and encountered longer days and more sunshine, but proving that theory is work for a geneticist rather than a wordfool.

Frisbee

Vikings didn't play with *frisbees* (as far as we know) but they did have a hand in the development of the name for them.

Back in the 1930s students at U.S. Middlebury College (and possibly Yale and Princeton too) began tossing around empty pie tins and the idea of the *frisbee* was born.

Frisbees became a registered trademark of the Wham-O Company in 1959. They had modelled the flying toy on the pie tins used by *Mrs. Frisbie's Pies* which were baked in Bridgeport, Connecticut. The spelling of the name was changed to avoid legal issues.

Frisbie was an old English surname, found in records as early as 1266 and associated with the Leicestershire town of *Frisby on the Wreak* which dates back to 1086 at least. The town name came from Old Danish and translated as the farmstead or village of the *Frisians*. *Frisian* is a word from Old Norse, *Frisa*, which describes a people and language along the North Sea coast in the general area of modern day Belgium.

Glitter

Perhaps it is unsurprising that plundering Vikings with a love of gold had a word for *glitter*, but it does summon up a charming image of a fierce bearded Viking with *glitter* on his cheeks.

Glitter entered English around 1300 spelled as *glideren*, from an earlier word *gliteren*, probably from a Scandinavian source. The most likely candidate is *glitra*, the Old Norse verb (to *glitter*).

Kilt

A *kilt* is the famous tartan skirt worn mostly by those hailing from Scotland, a word so linked to Scottish life that it's hard to believe it has Viking roots but don't forget, they landed there too and had a huge influence on the development of English, particularly in the northern areas of Britain.

A *kilt* was originally the part of the belted plaid which hung below the waist. The word entered Middle English in the mid 1300s as a verb, *kilten* (to tuck up) from a Scandinavian source, probably Old Norse *kilting* (shirt) and *kjalta* (fold made by gathering up to the knees). Danish also has *kilte* (to tuck up) and Swedish has *kilta* (to swaddle). Either way the piece of clothing known as a *kilt* got its name from its method of construction - the long piece of plaid being folded and tucked up with a belt for wearing.

The wearing of highland dress, including the *kilt*, was outlawed on the 1st of August 1746 in the aftermath of the Battle of Culloden and the Jacobite rising. The law was repealed in 1782.

Litmus

Every school science student performs a *litmus test* at some point and few of them realise they have the Vikings to thank. *Litmus* dye is naturally blue but turns red when exposed to acid and is restored to blue by alkaline exposure.

The idea of *litmus paper* dates to 1803 when it was created by the French chemist J.L. Guy-Lussac (1778-1850). He made many discoveries in his lifetime including recognising iodine as a new element, co-discovering boron, and establishing with Humboldt that water is made from two parts hydrogen and one part oxygen.

Litmus itself was used for the first time by Spanish physician Arnaldus de Villa Nova around 1300. Another Scandinavian link to *litmus* is that the pH scale (for measuring acidity and alkalinity of chemicals) was invented in 1909 by Soren Peder Pauritz Sorenson (1868-1939) who was a chemist in the Carlsberg Laboratory in Copenhagen, Denmark. The scale was known at the Sorenson scale until 1924 in his honour.

Litmus has a long history before the *litmus test*, however. It entered English in the early 1300s as *lit-mose*, a blue dye obtained from certain lichens. The word was formed from Old Norse building blocks – *lita* (to dye or stain) and *mos* (moss).

Murk

Murk has described gloomy darkness in English since the 1200s but was originally spelled as *myrke* thanks to its origins in Old Norse *myrkr* (darkness). *Myrkr* also provides *mørk* in Danish for the same notion.

Sometimes *murk* is spelled as *mirk*, especially in Scotland where *Mirk Monday* was the name given to a great solar eclipse on the 29th of March 1652. Astronomers had fun with names back in the day.

Again JRR Tolkien (1892-1973) dipped into Old Norse for the scary, and *murky*, *Mirkwood* forest in his book "The Hobbit". He wrote to his grandson that "*Mirkwood* is not an invention of mine" and explained its borrowing. *Mirkwood* was an anglicised form of the Norse name *Myrkvidr* or *mirkiwidu* from old anonymous Icelandic Edda poems describing a large forest dividing the land of the Goths from the land of the Huns.

Odd

Odd as the word for an uneven number arrived in the English dictionary around 1300 from the Old Norse word *oddi* (third or additional number). *Oddi* was used in Norse to describe an *odda-madr* – the third or *odd* man used to give a casting vote as well as *odd* numbers.

Oddi translated literally as a point of land and was related to triangles and the tips of weapons (often triangular in shape). Other Proto-Germanic originated languages had the same idea for a point or angle but only Norse developed it into the idea of three or *odd* numbers.

From 1400 *odd* could be used in English to denote something as being rare or renowned, but by the 1580s *odd* was referring to the strange and unusual in a more negative sense.

Odd job dates to the 1770s to explain a task which was not regular.

Plogging

Plogging isn't in the English dictionary, yet, but it deserves to be.

Scandinavian residents are deeply concerned about the effect of human activities on global climate change. Swedish activist Greta Thunberg is one well-known example. Another Swedish initiative also making waves is *plogging*.

Plogging started in Are, a ski resort. The idea is to combine jogging with picking up trash. The word is a combination of *jogging* and *plocka upp* (picking up). Trail runners bring a bag with them on their regular running session and gather litter as they go, binning it at the end of their route. It works as a combination of exercise and treasure hunt that leaves their environment cleaner afterwards.

Plogging has spread to countries like India and Mexico through the trail running community.

Scoff

Scoff, in the sense of mocking or making light of something, has been in English since the 1300s. It arrived from Old Norse *skaup* or *skop* (mockery or ridicule) and can also be seen in *skof* (Middle Danish). They may have their roots in the Proto-Germanic terms *skuf*, which also provides *scop*, the Old English word for poet.

Slang

Any writer on the topic of language will encounter the evolution of words from *slang* to mainstream phrases, and often the reverse process, but the origin of the word *slang* itself is worthy of study too.

Slang appeared in mainstream English around 1756 to denote the special vocabulary of "tramps or thieves" but by 1801 it was being used for the jargon associated with any particular profession and shortly thereafter it had the meaning it retains today – that of vivid, novel, informal language.

Slang changes almost daily, particularly amongst teens who'd die rather than admit their parental generation might understand their secret language because once they were young too (gasp, shock). Niche groups, group activities, incoming languages from visitors and migrants combine with pop culture to give new *slang* words to the dictionary. Some thrive, some die.

It's very appropriate then that *slang* itself came with a group of incomers who weren't approved of by mainstream society – the Vikings. Old Norse had the word *slangi* (tramp) and *slangr* (the straying of sheep). Norwegian has *slenge* (hang loose, dangle) and Danish has *slaenge* (to sling) plus derived words relating to a gang of people.

From those Scandinavian roots we get the northern England dialect word *slang* to describe a narrow piece of land running between other larger parcels of land. This led to the idea of *slang patter* (patter meaning talk in this case) which was associated with such lands.

This *slang patter* became linked over time with the people who lived on the *slang* lands, perhaps roving traders who camped there. Their colourful sales pitches and often rough language were the origin of *slang* in English.

One wonderful related American English word, *slangwhanger* (1807), hasn't survived and really should be revived. It meant a noisy or abusive writer or talker.

Slouch

A *slouch* as a lazy man sauntered slowly into English in the 1500s probably from a Scandinavian source, most likely Old Norse *slokr* (lazy fellow). The idea of *slouching* being a person with stooped head and shoulders didn't appear until the 1700s, around the time we acquired *slouch hats*.

Snape

If you're not a Harry Potter fan you can skip this entry, but if you are then you might be interested to hear *Professor Snape's* name has Viking roots. J.K. Rowling pays attention to how she names her characters and *Snape* is no exception.

Snape is an English verb from the early 1300s (also spelled *sneap*) and it means to be hard upon, to rebuke, revile, or snub. It comes from Old Norse *sneypa* which meant to outrage, dishonour, and disgrace possibly from similar sounding words about cutting, for example cutting timber to a fit a specific space.

Shakespeare, as he often does, got to the word long before Harry Potter. In "The Rape of Lucere" he talks about *sneaped* birds who were annoyed by a late frost.

Trash

Trash is viewed today as American English, due to its widespread usage in North America however it's an old word with Norse roots which pre-dates any English speaking people in North America.

Trash arrived in English in the late 1300s for things of little value, waste items probably from a Scandinavian origin. Old Norse had *tros* (rubbish, fallen leaves and twigs) while Norwegian has *trask* (lumber, *trash*) and Swedish has *trasa* (rags, tatters).

Shakespeare may have been an early user of the word to describe people rather than objects when he applied it to ill-bred groups of people in "Othello" in 1604. By 1831 *trash* was being used to describe poor whites in the southern states of the U.S.A..

Trash became domestic rubbish in 1906 in American English and led to *trash can* in 1914. During the 1900s the word became a verb too – *trashing* could be vandalism or destruction in the 1970s and *trash-talking* about a person arrived in the 1970s and 1980s.

Conclusion

After a year spent in the company of helmeted, bearded Vikings and their feisty womenfolk I can't help feeling that they have been unfairly represented in our school history books. The problem starts and ends with language.

Winston Churchill may have said "History is written by the victors" (note - he wasn't the first, early versions date to the 1700s) and the Vikings were the victors, but they didn't write the history. Although they won many battles and settled lands from Canada to Russia and Iceland to France, as well as ruling areas of the British Isles for nearly 800 years, ultimately they were replaced in their turn and the history of those centuries was written not by them but by Christian monks and rulers. The Anglo Saxon accounts of their interactions with the emerging English nation created bad press for the Vikings which they are still struggling to cast aside.

The same monks were raided by the Vikings at the start of their voyages to the British Isles so understandably they weren't happy about a bunch of people they regarded as heathens stealing their sacred objects (just gold to the Vikings), burning their abbeys, and taking the monks in slavery or death. Their vision of the raiders is what has largely persisted as history's judgement on the Norse farmers who sailed west in search of adventure, glory, and better land.

The Vikings weren't on a friendly summer tourist trip, that's certain, but what is often overlooked is that they did settle in Ireland, England, France, Russia, Iceland etc.

and lived fairly peacefully alongside the native people for centuries. Many changed religion and became so assimilated that somehow history doesn't remember them as Viking anymore. Technically all the achievements of the Normans are those of the Vikings for example, but once they settled in France that link is largely ignored.

Researching Viking history has left me yearning to visit Orkney, Shetland, and Iceland and see their lasting effect on the culture and landscape for myself. Festivals like Up Helly Aa and the oldest parliament in the world deserve to be seen for what they are – a legacy of a great people who were as influential as the Romans. The Romans, however, wrote their own histories, a smart move.

Sailing in small wooden boats with ambitious new designs and navigation techniques, the Vikings reached North America, they settled remote lands like Iceland for the first time, they established trade links right down to the Silk Road, they intermarried with ruling royal families of other nations, and established most of the coastal towns and cities of the British Isles. Along the way they gave the English language words from *akimbo* to *yule*.

The words in this book include the ones you would expect – *fjord, valhalla*, and *asgard*. Along with that I've included the words modern Scandinavian descendants of Vikings have added to English like *skype, bluetooth, IKEA*, and *lego*. Others sound so modern you would lay a bet that they couldn't have Norse roots and yet they do – *bug, awesome, mugging, kindle*, and *gun* are some examples of those.

While the large sailing vocabulary fits with our mental picture of the Vikings, the range of romantic words from *kiss* to *husband* and the legal and political words from *bylaw* to *ombudsman* expand that picture into a more accurate image of Viking life where law and order were important, family warmth mattered, and women had more freedom than anywhere else at the time.

In the end, after hunting through the English dictionary for Viking words, the ones I find most striking are the most simple. Pronouns like *they*, basic verbs like *get* and *take*, objects like *seat, rug,* and *window*. I don't speak Old Norse, but it has given the very core of everyday vocabulary to my mother tongue and I'm glad of that.

Perhaps if we remember the debt English owes to the Vikings, we can begin to see them with new eyes.

Thanks

Every week since 2009 I've played with unusual words on the Wordfoolery blog (https://wordfoolery.wordpress.com). A wonderful community of readers enrich the blog with word suggestions and their passion for language. Without them this book wouldn't exist.

A number of friends and fellow wordfools suggested words for inclusion in this book, you will see their names beside the words they suggested. Many thanks to MyNameIsTaken, Peter Sheehan, Rick Ellrod, and Brian Lynch. Thanks also to Noelle and Paddy for endless cake and encouragement, some of it virtual this time thanks to a certain virus.

Every November I take part in NaNoWriMo (National Novel Writing Month), as a writer and mentor to the Ireland NorthEast region which is filled with amazing writers of all ages and genres. NaNoWriMo 2019 saw me draft the first version of the book you're now reading. If you've ever thought of writing a book, I urge you to try NaNoWriMo at www.nanowrimo.org. You get a whole thirty days to write 50,000 words.

This book is dedicated to my Mum, a dedicated cruciverbalist who taught me how to *handsel* and *flit*, amongst other things.

Love and thanks always to Brendan, Daniel, and Eleanor.

References

Here's a selection of the resources I used to find and explore Viking words. Any mistakes are mine.

Special mention goes to Etymology Online (www.etymonline.com) which is a marvellous place for anybody with an interest in the English language. If you'd like a good introduction to Viking history try Neil Oliver's "Vikings". "Norse Mythology" by Neil Gaiman is a beautifully written starter guide to that topic.

- "Breverton's Nautical Curiosities" by Terry Breverton, 2010, Quercus (U.K.)
- "A Dictionary of Foreign Words & Phrases" by Tad Tuleja, 2009, Robert Hale (U.K.)
- "Sticklers, Sideburns & Bikinis" by Graeme Donald, 2008, Osprey Publishing (U.K.)
- "Words We Use" by Diarmuid Ó Muirithe, 2006, Gill & Macmillan (Ireland)
- "Planet Word" by JP Davidson, 2011, Michael Joseph (U.K.)
- "Vikings" by Neil Oliver, 2012, Weidenfeld & Nicolson (U.K.)
- "Norse Mythology" by Neil Gaiman, 2017, Bloomsbury Publishing (U.K.)
- "The Vikings – a Short History" by Martin Arnold, 2008, The History Press (U.K.)
- "Lagom: The Swedish Art of Balanced Living" by Linnea Dunne, 2017, Gaia (U.K.)
- "The Little Book of Snow" by Sally Coulthard, 2018, Head of Zeus (U.K.)

- www.etymonline.com
- www.wikipedia.org
- www.phrases.org.uk
- www.merriam-webster.com
- www.collinsdictionary.com
- www.dictionary.cambridge.org
- www.dictionary.com
- https://norse-mythology.org/cosmology/the-nine-worlds/helheim/
- https://www.history.com/news/10-things-you-may-not-know-about-the-Vikings
- https://www.thelocal.se/20170711/ten-words-you-didnt-know-came-from-the-Vikings-language-sweden
- https://www.printmag.com/article/who-named-the-kindle-and-why/
- https://historycollection.co/eight-facts-love-marriage-Viking-style/4/
- http://www.Viking.no/e/life/ewomen.htm
- https://en.natmus.dk/historical-knowledge/denmark/prehistoric-period-until-1050-ad/the-Viking-age/power-and-aristocracy/slaves-and-thralls/
- https://www.ancient-origins.net/history-famous-people/gunnhild-misidentified-bog-body-and-mother-kings-norse-sagas-005727
- https://warontherocks.com/2016/01/mead-and-the-Vikings/
- https://www.visitdenmark.com/denmark/highlights/hygge/what-hygge
- https://www.thevintagenews.com/2017/03/21/the-Vikings-sold-narwhal-tusks-as-unicorn-horns/
- http://www.Viking.no/e/orkney/
- https://www.rte.ie/news/newslens/2019/0426/1045803-plogging-in-sweden/
- https://www.shetland.org/about/history

- https://www.historyonthenet.com/Viking-law-and-government-the-thing
- https://norse-mythology.org/cosmology/valhalla/
- https://www.telegraph.co.uk/finance/newsbysector/retailandconsumer/9643122/Ikea-25-facts.html
- https://www.bbc.co.uk/programmes/articles/2W5jzMw4DFDCvP3jsFKcgQJ/ways-you-talk-like-a-Viking-every-day
- https://icelandmag.is/article/Vikings-left-their-mark-european-map-here-our-guide-help-you-find-them
- http://www.shieldmaidenssanctum.com/blog/2019/2/25/what-is-a-shieldmaiden

About the Author

Grace Tierney is a columnist, author, and blogger writing on Ireland's coast. She is the Ireland North East organiser for National Novel Writing Month (www.NaNoWriMo.org) and actually enjoys the challenge of writing 50,000 words in one month. She blogs about unusual words at http://wordfoolery.wordpress.com, tweets @Wordfoolery, and serialises contemporary comic fiction at www.channillo.com.

Her other books about words include "How To Get Your Name In The Dictionary" (the extraordinary lives of those who gave their names as eponyms to English), and "Words The Sea Gave Us" (nautical nouns from fishermen, pirates, and explorers). She also broadcasts a monthly slot about the history of words on LMFM radio.

Her favourite Viking words are *hug* (because it is so unexpected that we'd get that from a group of plunderers) and *attercop* because it's from her favourite childhood book.

https://twitter.com/Wordfoolery - writing / life
www.facebook.com/gracetierneywriter - writing / life
www.instagram.com/wordfoolery/ – history photos
www.pinterest.co.uk/GraceTierneyIrl/ - crafts, writing, history

If You Enjoyed This Book

Grace blogs every week about the history of unusual words on Wordfoolery (http://wordfoolery.wordpress.com). Drop by, all word-lovers are welcome. She takes requests so if you have a favourite obscure word, suggest it.

The easiest way to thank an author of any book, but especially one who wears the indie-publisher hat, is to post an honest review. It makes a huge difference to the visibility of the book and future sales, so if you enjoyed this romp through Norse nouns and Viking verbs, please take a couple of minutes to review it. Thank you so much.

If you like Viking history you'll find a free download called **"Nine Things You Never Knew About Vikings"** on the Wordfoolery download page. It explains how the Vikings discovered North America before Columbus, didn't wear horned helmets, have the oldest parliament in the world, ruled Britain longer than the Romans, and are related to the Danish royal family. (https://wordfoolery.wordpress.com/downloads/)

Index

Burn	139
-by	96
Bylaw	59
Cake	9
Calf	92
Call	139
Cart	34
Cast	140
Celsius	105
Clip	34
Club	119
Copenhagen	96
Cosy	141
Crawl	141
Crook	35
Cross	178
Crow's Nest	19
Dale	96
Dandruff	193
Dappled	142
Dock	20
Die	120
Dint	120
Dirt	35
Drag	142
Dream	178
Dregs	10
Droopy	193
Earl	60
Eddy	21
Egg	10
Eiderdown	143
Enthrall	46
Fell	170
Fellow	47
Ferry	21
Fjord	170

Harbour	22
Haven	22
Heathen	182
Hell	184
Helm	23
Helmet	123
Hit	124
Holm	172
Honeymoon	52
Hug	52
Hurry	147
Husband	53
Hustings	63
Hygge	105
Iceland	98
IKEA	106
Ill	92
Irk	147
Keel	23
Keg	12
Kid	77
Kilt	195
Kindle	107
Kirk	185
Kiss	53
Knacker	36
Knell	148
Knife	124
Knit	148
Knoll	172
Knot	24
Kraken	78
Lagom	107
Lass & Lad	54
Law	64
Leg	92
Lego	108

Raise	153
Ram	79
Rambo	125
Ransack	126
Reef and Reefer	27
Reindeer	80
Reykjavik	101
Rim	174
Root	38
Rotten	12
Rug & Rugged	153
Russia	101
Saga	85
Sale	154
Scales	12
Scant	154
Scarborough	102
Scare	127
Scathe	128
Scoff	199
Scold	68
Score	39
Scrap	154
Scrape	155
Scrub	155
Scythe	38
Seat	155
Seemly	55
Sheet	27
Shetland	102
Shield Maiden	128
Shrimp	81
Skep	40
Ski	155
Skid	130
Skill	156
Skin	93

Have You Read Grace Tierney's Other Books?

"How To Get Your Name In The Dictionary" (2018)

A light-hearted look at the lives of the soldiers, inventors, style icons, and villains who gave their names to the English language as eponyms. From atlas to zeppelin English is full of words named for Greek gods, explorers, serious scientists, and crafty chefs. These heroes and heroines, scattered through world history, all did something extraordinary to squeeze their name into the dictionary, and this book celebrates their biographies.

More than **260 eponyms** are featured across subjects as diverse as food, Irish history, calendars, hats, inventions, words named after places, Greek gods, military history, politics, astronomy, fashion, popular phrases, villains, science, and a selection of eponyms which simply defy categorisation.

Ideal for word geeks, history lovers, and biography buffs.

"Words The Sea Gave Us" (2020)

From *baggywinkle* and *gollywobbler* to *tempest* and *flotsam*, the sea in all her moods added a boatload of words to the English language throughout history. Cast your line for the maritime origins of *skyscraper, mollgogger, strike, cyber*, along with phrases like *getting hitched, red herring, hot pursuit*, and *taking them down a peg*.

Explore parts of a ship, sail names, crew titles, surfer slang, marine monsters, nautical navigation, flying the flag, and of course, how to talk like a Scurvy Pirate. Gather sea fables, fashions, and weather and you'll be ready to set sail.

Previous nautical experience not required.

Ideal for word geeks, beachcombers, and nautical history buffs.

Coming Soon in the Words Series!

- "Words Christmas Gave Us"
- "Words The Weather Gave Us"
- "Words The French Gave Us"
- "Words The War Gave Us"
- "Words The Greeks Gave Us"
- "Words The Romans Gave Us"
- "Words Publishing Gave Us"
- "Words The Germans Gave Us"

"The Librarian's Secret Diary"

Nina is the new librarian on the block. She's learning the shelves with her buzzword-spouting boss and the senior librarian who hates reading and can't wait to retire.

She records the crazy reader requests and the knitting group in-fighting in her secret diary while trying to get the printer to work, flirting with the inter-library-loan guy, and struggling to discover why their romance books are acquiring red pen marks on page five.

Available to read on www.Channillo.com, the subscription reading platform (think Netflix for books). First chapter is free to read.

"Hamster Stew & Other Stories" (2017) is a diary-style comedy serial about the adventures of an Irish mom, Trish McTaggart, struggling with her teenage son, a scary ten year old daughter, and an out of control life which lurches from disaster to chaos.

All she wants is a part-time job, more passion with her Scottish husband, and a hands-off mother-in-law but life, and her daughter, are conspiring against her dreams. Perhaps the lessons her friend is giving her in "how to say no" will help?

Available to read on www.Channillo.com, the subscription reading platform (think Netflix for books). First chapter is free to read.

"Nit Roast & Other Stories" (2018) is a first person, diary-style comedy serial about the adventures of an Irish mom.

Trish McTaggart's family life is still a mess. Her diary holds her worries – an animal-obsessed daughter, a teen son drinking, an absent-minded husband, and a local parent who's out to get her. Building her new sewing business will be the easy part this year. This is a sequel to "Hamster Stew & Other Stories".

Available to read on www.Channillo.com, the subscription reading platform (think Netflix for books). First chapter is free to read.

Printed in Poland
by Amazon Fulfillment
Poland Sp. z o.o., Wrocław

80670251R00128